Memoirs of a Lightkeeper's Son

– Life on St. Paul Island –

Billy Budge

Pottersfield Press, Lawrencetown Beach, Nova Scotia, Canada

© Copyright 2003 Billy Budge

National Library of Canada Cataloguing in Publication

Budge, Billy, 1948-

    Memoirs of a lightkeeper's son / Billy Budge.

ISBN 1-895900-61-1

1. Budge, Billy, 1948- —Childhood and youth. 2. St. Paul Island (N.S.) —
Biography. 3. Lighthouse keepers—Nova Scotia—St. Paul Island. I. Title.

FC2345.S25Z49 2003   971.6'9   C2003-904496-3

Cover design: Dalhousie Graphics

Cover photo: Billy Budge

Pottersfield Press acknowledges the support of the Canada Council for the
Arts. We acknowledge the financial support of the Government of Canada
through the Book Publishing Industry Development Program for our publishing activities. We also acknowledge the support of the Novs Scotia Department of Tourism and Culture, Cultural Affairs Division.

Pottersfield Press
83 Leslie Road
East Lawrencetown
Nova Scotia, Canada, B2Z 1P8
Website: www.pottersfieldpress.com
To order, phone toll-free 1-800-NIMBUS9 (1-800-646-2879)
Printed in Canada

To Edith, Fred and Ina Budge

Acknowledgements

A special thanks to my friend John Nickelson, who gave me inspiration and encouragement to continue writing. A sincere appreciation to my editor Shelly Porter, for the hours she spent working with me on the manuscript. Thanks also to Stan Cairns, Merlyn Baker, John Gatza, Duane Traver, Don Young, Bob Martin's Photographic Studio, and all others who have contributed in any way.

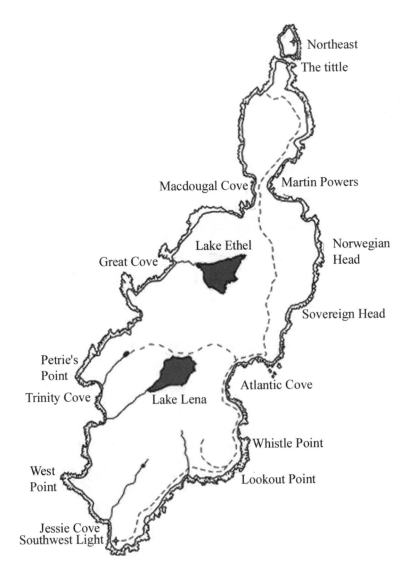

Northeast

The tittle

Macdougal Cove

Martin Powers

Lake Ethel

Norwegian
Head

Great Cove

Sovereign Head

Petrie's
Point

Atlantic Cove

Trinity Cove

Lake Lena

Whistle Point

West
Point

Lookout Point

Jessie Cove
Southwest Light

St. Paul Island

1

The Letter

It was a calm morning in early June 1955, the silence broken only by strange sounds drifting in from the ocean. I paused briefly to glance toward the source of the noise echoing off the windows of our house. It was a distinct snapping sound, similar to wine corks popping several times a second. A visitor to Neil's Harbour, our small village in Cape Breton, Nova Scotia, might find this noise unusual but to the locals it was a part of everyday life.

Peering through the narrow band of trees between the shoreline and the roadway, I caught a glimpse of shapes moving along the horizon. Lobster season was in full force. Fisherman were out in their small boats pulling their traps, harvesting the lobsters that would later be sold at the nearby fish-processing plant.

If there was still any doubt as to the origin of those sounds, a person would have only to look into the engine room of one of the small boats. In the year 1955, car engines or other multicylinder motors were not widely used in these small craft. They relied upon a marine engine that fishermen called a "make and break," or a "one-lunger." These engines consisted of one oversized cylinder and an exterior flywheel to which was attached a permanent crank handle. The simplicity of their construction made them very reliable, and usually it only required one manual jerk on the crank to start the motor. The slow beat of the piston, and the resultant loud snapping sound from the exhaust pipe, could be heard for miles. The whole Neil's Harbour fleet, snapping along and out of synch with one another, awakened me that morning.

I was too young to be a fisherman, or to even be of much help in the boat. Yet a boy of seven still has chores to do. At home, I hauled buckets of water from the nearby well for drinking and other household purposes. I fed King, our big Newfoundland dog, and carried in coal for cooking and heating. Dad said that the easiest way to remember the chores was to say aloud, "Coal, water, and cod heads" – cod heads were food for the dog.

Weekdays, I attended school. At the time, our school in Neil's Harbour was not like an ordinary school. Several classes, including mine of Grade One, were without a teacher. At least, we were without a *licensed* teacher. That year the local school board was unsuccessful in acquiring any professional teachers. It fell to a few ambitious village ladies to try to conduct classes. Since these women had no authority to correct papers or to give grades, all school work was evaluated via correspondence. These amateur teachers taught the lessons to the best of their ability, then mailed each student's papers to a provincial education centre in the city of Halifax, almost three hundred miles away. In Halifax, examiners graded the material and returned it to the school. Our local ladies put forth their best effort and we learned well. None of us ever realized they were not licensed teachers.

On this Saturday morning my mother had a special errand for me.

"Billy," she said, "will you go to the post office and pick up our mail?"

Our post office was not more than half a mile from home, just beyond the boat dock.

"Yes, Mom," I said, seizing the opportunity to visit my friends, who would be playing down by the pier. My mother was always concerned about me hanging around the wharf, but she never seemed to mind if I was a little late returning with the mail.

"Is that all the mail there is today, Aunt Ella?" I asked, as she handed me a single envelope. My aunt, also the postmistress, just nodded her head and smiled. I thanked her and stepped out the door of the small plywood hut (our new post office). From the post office, I could clearly see the dock on the other side of the cove. In the still morning air I could hear echos of laughter from the fishermen who were busy unloading their catches of lobsters.

A series of fishing shacks were clustered around the pier. One in particular seemed to attract a lot of attention. A group of men were sitting on an old, weather-beaten log alongside it. Some of them were quite old and no longer fished, while others had finished fishing for the day. They would often sit there for hours whittling, chewing tobacco and telling stories. "Braggy" always seemed to spin the best yarns, holding everyone's attention for the longest time. Normally I would have paused to linger and listen, but on that day, for some reason, I chose not to stop. I headed home with the single brown envelope clutched in my hand, totally unaware that the letter inside would dramatically change the lives of everyone in our family forever.

I had almost reached our driveway when I saw my father and a friend walking toward me. Father was carrying a bucket in his hand. As he drew closer I could see that the bucket was filled with lobsters, fresh from the wharf.

"Take these lobsters and give them to your mother. I'll be back shortly," he said and turned to walk away.

"Before you go, Dad," I said, "I have a letter here for you."

His face paled as he took the letter from my hand. He turned to his friend saying, "Jim, I'm scared to death to open this brown envelope."

He tore it open and began to read. I could see his face light up as he folded the letter and placed it back inside the envelope. Beaming with excitement, he turned to Jim and said, "I got the job!"

Since his return from World War II in March 1946, my father had not had steady employment. Continuous work was almost impossible to find. Over the past nine years, Dad had tried his hand at various jobs, none of which was permanent or without hardships. He longed for a job with a future and was determined to settle for nothing less. Could it be, finally, he was holding in his hand the answer to his dreams? Dad remembered coming home from the war, taking that first job fishing with his uncle in a small boat. Fish catches were down that year. Money was scarce for fishermen, even more so for a fisherman's helper. When things proved no better the following year, something had to change.

Although times were bad, Cupid was still at work. My father fell in love with a local girl; they married in 1947. Her name was Edith Petrie, and she would later become my mother. She walked with a distinctive limp, the result of polio, but her disability never seemed to impede her ability to move nor to enjoy life. She always said that she was lucky to have survived: polio had claimed the lives of many of her childhood friends.

The following year, 1948, my father assumed responsibility for two dependents: my mother, and me, born on January 25. Things seemed to be going from bad to worse!

Around this time, my father heard a rumour about a boat for sale. The prospect of owning his own boat seemed too good an opportunity to let pass. Forty-two feet long with a narrow beam, she was carvel-planked and constructed with wood from mainland Nova Scotia. Powered by two car engines mounted side by side, this boat was faster than many of the others in the local fleet. She was named, appropriately, *Fade Away*.

After a deal was reached, my father prepared the boat for the sword-fishing season. His brother, Walter, was his only crewman. Swordfishing was more like hunting than fishing: the fish had to be spotted visually on the surface, harpooned, and drowned before it could be landed aboard the boat. It was somewhat like whaling, except on a smaller scale. My father and Uncle Walter pursued the elusive swordfish for several seasons and did fairly well, even though the fish were worth only a few cents a pound. Their best catch was five fish in one day; often they caught only two or three fish a week. They were barely making ends meet. In swordfishing, good weather is critical. For best results, the fishermen hope for what they call "oily calm" water. Under these conditions a swordfish fin, the only part of the fish visible in the water, could be seen at a great distance. But calm seas and light winds seldom prevail in northern Atlantic latitudes, and the season my father swordfished was no calmer than any other.

My father pursued several other kinds of fishing over the next five years. The hook-and-line cod fishery offered the best earning potential. It could last from early spring until Christmas, when severe cold and drift ice from the Gulf of St. Lawrence forced the fishermen to haul their boats ashore and quit for the season. But cod fishing too had its pitfalls. Frequently, there were no fish buyers in the immediate area. My father's catches had to be transported a long distance up the coast just to be sold. This proved costly for the fisherman.

My father often wondered if the effort to continue was worthwhile. Fishing is a dangerous life as well: storms spring up without warning, and my mother worried about my father, still out on the water. It seemed that fishing offered only hardships to those determined to remain at it. Eventually, after careful consideration, and seeing nothing in the immediate future that looked even remotely bright in earning a living from the sea, my father decided to quit fishing. In the fall of 1953, he tied the *Fade Away* to the wharf in Dingwall for the last time.

Meanwhile, things were beginning to happen in the interior of Cape Breton. The Government of Canada was involved in further development of the national park on the northern section of the island. With its spectacular, rugged cliffs and mountainous terrain, this region of Cape Breton offered excellent potential for tourism. The Cape Breton Highlands National Park was first established in the late 1930s. My father was employed with the park building roads in 1939, prior to his departure for the war in Europe. Now, in 1953, new roads had to be constructed, campgrounds created, and hiking trails developed to attract and serve visitors. My father, realizing that workers would be required to complete these tasks, applied for employment.

He was successful in being hired, this time with the understanding that it would be a permanent, full-time position. He could make plans for the future with a steady income guaranteed at last. He was employed as a labourer. Each day, he worked with a crew cutting hiking trails and building small bridges. There was a feeling of optimism among the men: perhaps these jobs could last indefinitely. Then, as the crew reported for work one cold morning in late fall, they received the news that everyone was being laid off for the winter. Once again, my father was forced to live with part-time, seasonal employment. During his time off work, he received unemployment insurance payments from the Canadian government, only a few dollars each month.

In the spring of 1955, while working part time as a bartender at the Neil's Harbour Royal Canadian Legion, he noticed a job posting on the bulletin board for a lighthouse keeper. It stated that a preference would be given to war veterans. Immediately, he applied. Now, less than a month later, he was holding the affirmative response in his hand. Smiling to his friend he said, "Yes, Jim, I'm going to be the lighthouse keeper at the Southwest light station on St. Paul Island!"

Stuffing the envelope into his coat pocket, he looked at me. "Now, Billy, let's go home and tell Mom."

I had no idea where St. Paul Island was located, but that didn't dampen my enthusiasm. I burst into the kitchen yelling, "Hey, Mom! We're going to St. Paul Island!"

Mom dropped the dishcloth she was holding, and staggered backwards against the wall.

"Oh, my God!" she said.

2

An Island to Shun

My mother's reaction to our impending move to St. Paul Island indicated that it was not just a simple move to another neighbourhood. She knew it meant a dramatic change in lifestyle. Although I was somewhat excited about moving, I did not feel there would be any major changes that should concern me. After all, to my child's mind, it did not appear that we would be moving very far. But a short distance across the ocean is vastly different from an equal distance down the highway.

One clear Sunday afternoon shortly after my father received the letter, Grandfather and I walked to Lighthouse Point in Neil's Harbour. He sat on a rock just beyond the lighthouse and looked out over the ocean through his binoculars. After studying the sea for a few moments, he lowered the binoculars and pointed to a small grey hump on the northeastern horizon.

"That's St. Paul Island out there, Billy," he said. "That's where you're going to be living."

Even though it was a very clear day, and I squinted hard to catch a glimpse of my future home, I could not clearly see what lay there. I had

St. Paul Island with Southwest Point in the foreground at the bottom of the photo. The well-defined cove on the right side of the photo is Atlantic Cove with Lake Lena immediately beside it. The tractor trail that once skirted the shoreline and ran along the cliffs between the cove and the Southwest Light has long since been recelaimed by nature and is no longer visible. (Billy Budge photo)

no knowledge of the island's historic past, nor was I aware of its present situation. I did know that soon a government supply ship would be coming from Halifax to pick up our family with all our belongings, and transport us to that distant place.

St. Paul Island, less than two square miles in area, rises out of the sea about thirteen miles northeast of Cape North, and is the northern-most part of Nova Scotia. The island is barely three miles long and about one mile across at its widest point. It's situated in the Cabot Strait, that body of water which separates Cape Breton and Newfound-land.

The Cabot Strait deals harshly with this small piece of land that dares to sit within its grasp. Strong currents sweep the island with the changing tides of the Gulf of St. Lawrence. During the winter months, a region of the Gulf east of the St. Lawrence River freezes, forming heavy ice ten to twenty feet thick. Wind and sea break off portions of this ice mass, which float away as huge pans. This process of freezing and breaking away eventually fills the whole Gulf of St. Lawrence with "drift ice." Although individual pans of ice can cover several square miles, they must not be confused with icebergs, which are broken-off sections of a glacier. Strong tides and the prevailing winds of the Gulf and the Cabot Strait move this large body of drift ice toward the open Atlantic. Around mid-January, the first ice floes reach St. Paul Island. They scrape and grind past the granite cliffs, thundering by like a never-ending train. If cold temperatures persist throughout the winter, it could be late May before the last sheet floats past.

The island is covered with thick, stunted spruce forest, with a few small grassy areas near the shore. Some hardwood trees grow among the evergreens, but most die before they become very large. Most of the island's plants, high atop cliffs of solid granite, are protected from the direct force of the sea.

Yet St. Paul Island offers little protection for the weary sailor seeking shelter from a passing storm. Ocean swells roll over jagged reefs; waves curl and crash against a solid coast of vertical cliffs and deep crevasses. There are a few pebble beaches, but no sand anywhere. There is no protected harbour where a boat could anchor and wait for the weather to improve. There are two or three small coves that offer some shelter from certain winds, but the island's northeast-southwest orientation means there is no shelter from a nor-easter. Winter gales often last for several days, or even for a week.

The waters off St. Paul Island are strewn with shipwrecks. Early maps of the island were not reliable and this may have contributed to some wrecks. St. Paul was inaccurately shaped on some early charts, and often incorrectly located. Most often the mishap was a result of the ship being driven off course in a storm, and poor visibility. There are as many as sixty known and recorded shipwrecks. There is no way of knowing how many ships were lost in storms with no one surviving to tell the tale. A local diver and historian, Alex Storm, has done extensive research and diving around St. Paul. He feels the actual number of shipwrecks may be triple the number of those recorded. In some places, divers have discovered the remains of one shipwreck on top of another.

St. Paul Island delivered cruel punishment to sailors whose ship's captain made an error in calculations. A ship sailing through the Cabot Strait in early winter might well encounter raging seas and gale-force winds. Without warning, out of the blinding snow, a solid vertical wall of rock would appear, towering over the ship. Since these early sailing vessels could not stop or turn quickly, they sailed, to their doom, onto a reef hidden beneath the raging surf. The passengers and crew were forced to abandon ship and attempt to reach the island. Depending on where the ship ran aground, the chances of reaching shore would range from difficult to impossible. The strong currents, pounding surf, and jagged rocks would claim the lives of many before they could even reach land. Furthermore, it would require special equipment to scale some of the cliffs.

Those able to reach shore would soon find themselves in peril on the land. Prior to 1832, St. Paul Island was uninhabited. There was no human assistance or structures where survivors could seek shelter. There is no record of how many lives were lost due to drowning, freezing or starving to death on the island.

The worst recorded marine disaster on St. Paul Island was the loss of the *Royal Sovereign* in October of 1814. She was a British transport ship loaded with troops bound from Quebec to England after the War of 1812-1814. The ship encountered an easterly gale while still in the Gulf of St. Lawrence. She lasted only a few minutes after striking a reef near the northern end of St. Paul. Only thirty-seven people who survived the tragedy lived long enough to be evacuated. More than two hundred others either went down with the wreck or died later on shore.

One wreck, whose fate is well documented, brought about the first rescue development on St. Paul Island. The *Jessie*, a barque out of Prince Edward Island, ran aground on the Southwest Point on January 1, 1825. The crew and passengers reached the shore safely and constructed a makeshift shelter. Their fires could be seen at night from the village of Cape North, but drift ice and strong currents prevented anyone going to their rescue. They all starved to death over the winter. In the spring, a diary was recovered that gave a vivid account of their ordeal, right up until the last few hours of life. The ship's owner, Mr. Mackay, the last to die, made the final entry in the diary on the 17th of March. In the spring of that year fishermen from Cheticamp found the remains of those who perished and recovered the diary.

This tragedy generated a great deal of publicity. The governments of Nova Scotia and New Brunswick realized that something must be done with this island nature had treacherously placed in the shipping lane. In 1832, each of these provinces built a lifesaving station on St.

Paul. The Nova Scotia station was established at Atlantic Cove on the eastern side; New Brunswick chose Trinity Cove, on the western side. The crew from each station, provisioned with equipment to rescue and care for shipwreck survivors, patrolled the island daily. Even with the lifesaving stations in place, a shipwrecked person's chances of survival were still slim. Any ship that ran aground during the night would not be discovered until dawn, at the earliest. If the storm was severe, a wooden ship would last only an hour or two before the surf battered it to splinters against the jagged ledges of the island. Many times, the shore patrol discovered nighttime wrecks too late to be of any assistance.

Ships that were wrecked during the daylight hours did not fare much better. The same waves destroying the grounded craft also prevented the launching of lifeboats from the beach. If a cable could not be secured between the ship and the shore, there was little that could be done toward saving lives. In such cases, the lifesaving crew could only watch helplessly as the passengers and crew were swept into the sea. In the days that followed they would undertake the gruesome task of burying the dead as the bodies washed ashore. Sometimes the bodies numbered in the hundreds and were buried in mass graves. St. Paul Island soon become known as the "Graveyard of the Gulf."

In 1838, the British government dispatched Samuel Cunard (founder of Cunard Steamship Lines) to St. Paul Island to find a suitable site to erect a lighthouse. On this assignment Mr. Cunard was accompanied by John Campbell. Campbell was already resident in Nova Scotia, having emigrated from Scotland with his family . These men decided that two lighthouses should be built on the island, one at the northeast end and another at the southwest. The following year John Campbell was appointed Governor of St. Paul Island, with the responsibility of supervising the construction of the lighthouses and overseeing the operation of the two lifesaving stations. It took more than a year to complete construction. Shortly before Christmas 1840, both lighthouses were in operation.

John Campbell served as Governor for nineteen years, living on the island with his wife and children. During that time there were twelve shipwrecks, with 161 lives lost. Most of those perished on one ship, the *Palace,* bound from England to Quebec with three hundred passengers.

Mr. Campbell and his lifesaving crew managed to save half the people on board before the ship disintegrated, sending the remainder to a watery grave. In 1874, John Campbell's son, Samuel, was appointed Governor of St. Paul Island. He served there until about 1914. Several of his children were born on the island; its lakes bear the names of two of his daughters, Ethel and Lena.

Although the lighthouses and lifesaving stations were a major improvement in safety, shipwrecks continued to occur. Lighthouses were effective only on clear nights; they were of little use in poor visibility associated with storms and fog. Conditions would not improve dramatically until the early twentieth century, when ships became equipped with more modern navigational equipment.

In 1918, a Newfoundland businessman established a lobster cannery on the western side of the island. The population swelled, and the island bustled with activity. At the peak of the lobster season the cannery employed as many as fifty workers. Many of the employees came from Neil's Harbour and other northern Cape Breton communities. In the evenings there would be parties and dances attended by the factory workers, the lifesaving crews, and the lighthouse keepers with their families. The lobster cannery operated only in the summer. When the season was past, all the workers returned to their homes on the mainland.

By the time the cannery closed in 1920, safety and navigation around St. Paul had vastly improved. In 1924, a wireless station began operating at Atlantic Cove, providing communication with the outside world. Telegraph operators came with their families, and for a time lived with the lifesaving crew. The operators were required to send daily weather reports and, during the winter months, drift ice conditions. Marine incidents would be reported to a rescue centre in North Sydney. The Northeast light station was now equipped with a foghorn, replacing a steam whistle that had been installed earlier on the southern side of Atlantic Cove. With this updated equipment, a passing mariner could not only see the light and hear the foghorn, but could also communicate with the station operator.

In 1925, the Canadian government decided that the lifesaving stations on St. Paul Island were no longer necessary and closed them down. These stations had served mariners well for ninety-three years; now politicians felt that modern equipment made the likelihood of major shipwrecks extremely remote. The safety of marine navigation could be assured with a lighthouse at either end and a wireless station in the middle.

New technologies were added as they became available. A radio beacon, which provided a navigational fix to ships and planes, was installed at the wireless station in the late 1940s. Generators were installed at around the same time, providing the station with electricity.

Even as my grandfather and I were standing on Neil's Harbour Point on that August day in 1955, more changes were being planned for St. Paul Island. Only months after we were due to arrive, the wireless station at Atlantic Cove would also be closed down and vacated. After that, our family would be alone on the island except for the folks at the other light station, who were isolated from us.

The lighthouse on the northeastern end of St. Paul Island is not located on the main island. It is situated on a smaller island composed of a few acres of grass and rock. It is separated from the main island by a narrow channel about a hundred feet wide known as a "tittle." Strong currents flow through the channel, pausing only briefly during the changing of the tides. This small island, called the "Northeast," was connected to the main island by a device known as a boatswain chair. It consisted of a box, or chair, suspended by pulleys from a cable attached to a tower on either side of the channel. A person would sit in the chair and pull themselves across with a rope.

Even though the two lighthouses were only three miles apart, the lightkeepers seldom visited one another. The island's dense growth of stunted trees, steep slopes, jagged rocks, and, in the winter, the ice and snow, made travel difficult. A few times during the summer when the weather permitted, the lightkeepers visited each other by boat.

Conditions at the Southwest lighthouse, our destination, were entirely different from those at the Northeast lighthouse. There was no electricity for our house and no generators to operate the light. My father would not have any assistant keepers because our station did not have a radio beacon or foghorn that required extra crew for its management. Although it was a one-man operation, activating the light was a fairly complex procedure. An even more demanding task was seeing that it remained functional throughout the night. However, our greatest challenge as a family would be learning to live together without friends or neighbours.

On the other hand, perhaps we would not be completely alone. Many previous St. Paul Island dwellers claimed that the island was haunted. Ghosts were frequently reported, especially in or near the dwelling house on the Southwest. Many people felt the ghosts were the spirits of sailors or passengers from past shipwrecks who were unhappy with their untimely death, and could not find peace in their final resting place. Perhaps my enthusiasm would have been somewhat subdued if I had known what my mother knew. It would appear that my father had made a choice for us to leave civilization and go live in self-imposed exile. Many people would have regarded St. Paul as an island to shun, but as a seven-year-old boy, I could not wait to get there.

3

All Aboard – Well, Half Anyway

Our departure time was fast approaching. The office of the Canadian Department of Transportation in Halifax had recently advised my father to be prepared to leave on or near the first of September. A number of concerns had to be addressed and resolved before the arrival of that date. When it was time to go, the government supply ship *Lady Laurier* would drop its anchor off Neil's Harbour and send a launch ashore to pick up our family and our possessions.

There was one thing that I had already taken care of on my own. At the closing of the school year in June, the teacher asked me to explain to the class what kind of school I would be attending in the fall on St. Paul Island.

"You see, Teacher, there are no schools on the island," I explained, holding back the urge to grin over such a serious shortcoming. "I'll be studying at home and doing my school work by correspondence."

I went on to say that my dad intended to remain on the island for perhaps as long as five years. If that happened, the next time I attended school I would be in grade seven. After sharing my excitement about St. Paul with the class, I said goodbye, having completed only grade one.

It was now up to my parents to oversee my schoolwork. A meeting was arranged with the school superintendent, wherein all necessary books and papers were acquired for correspondence studies. Even my four-year-old sister, Ina, was enrolled for studies in the upcoming school year: she would begin first grade then. For some reason, my father felt that she should begin school at this early age, even though the regulations stated that the starting age for school was six.

Many people frown upon the use of correspondence as a form of education. Too often the flexibility of such a system leads to neglect, which often results in the student lagging academically and having problems when returning to the regular classroom. This drawback concerned both my parents. They had heard stories of children who, after several years of correspondence studies, were not prepared to enter their expected grade when they again enrolled in a public school.

The school board had given us the proper material for an adequate education. All else that was required was a commitment to learn, and some degree of honesty. It would be up to all of us, the two teachers and two students, to ensure that the lessons were read and understood and the assignments completed. With help from instructions in the teacher's guide, most lessons were completed in our notebooks and corrected by my father. A small percentage was sent to Halifax to be corrected by provincial examiners. If there was any misunderstanding regarding lessons, there was no one outside the family to turn to for help. With a thorough knowledge of what was expected, we accepted all the books and papers, and packed them away for the voyage.

Packing operations were now getting under way in earnest. It was difficult to know just what items to pack and which ones to leave behind. We would be responsible for shipping; there would be no movers coming to do the job for us. My dad and I made several trips to the local store for cardboard boxes in which to pack the smaller things. My mother carefully wrapped all the fragile items and packed them away herself. Sadly, many of her favourite possessions would not be coming with us. We already knew there was no electricity in our new home, so it was useless to pack any item that came with a plug. I did notice her slip two of her prized electric lamps into one of the boxes. I guess she must have thought they would look good sitting on her end tables, even though she could never turn them on.

My grandfather often came to help, bringing his hammer and saw. A skilled carpenter, he built wooden crates in which to ship the heavier items. He was eager to let me assist him with the nailing: he wanted me to become a carpenter when I grew up. He knew that he would not be able to visit us often, if ever, on St. Paul Island. The thought saddened him greatly. On more than one occasion I saw him stop to wipe away a tear that had trickled down his cheek.

September was quickly approaching. With all the packing complete, there was little left to do except wait for the ship. Then Dad received word that the *Lady Laurier* would be delayed due to stormy weather on Sable Island. Heavy surf was making it difficult to land supplies for the lighthouse stations there. The ship would not leave until the last item was placed ashore. We would have to be ready to leave at a moment's notice.

Meanwhile, at home we were more or less camping out. We slept on the floor, and when meal time came, we ate in a picnic style. It was fun for a while, but soon everyone became restless. We grew more impatient with each passing day. We kept a constant vigil toward the sea, though it was not necessary: Neil's Harbour was a small community with no secrets. Everyone was watching with us.

One day, Ina seemed to be having a little more discomfort than the rest of us in coping with the situation. My mother was concerned about Ina's uneasiness, but saw no cause for alarm. The following day, however, it was apparent that Ina was ill. She had stomach pain and was running a fever. I went along with my parents that evening when they took her to the doctor. They hoped a little medicine would cure her illness.

My father and I waited outside as my mother carried Ina into the doctor's office. When Mother emerged a few moments later, the look on her face told us that something was terribly wrong.

"Freddy," she said, "Ina is suffering from an inflamed appendix. I'll have to leave tonight and take her to the hospital in North Sydney. The doctor has made arrangements for surgery to be performed early tomorrow morning."

The government supply ship *Lady Laurier.*

Transportation was arranged immediately. My mother and Ina sped off into the night, leaving Dad and me standing on the side of the road. We walked home to await word from the hospital, and to watch for the ship.

Our wait for the *Lady Laurier* was brief. Someone came to our door early the next morning to tell us that black smoke was visible on the horizon. The *Lady Laurier* was a coal-fired, steam-driven ship: smoke from the stack could be seen long before the ship appeared. Dad had arranged for the use of a large truck and immediately he summoned the driver. The truck was quickly backed into our driveway. One of our neighbours came along to help with the loading of all our worldly goods. Soon everything was piled up on the truck. As the truck moved slowly down the driveway, our neighbour climbed high atop the load and laid across one of our mattresses. I envied him, way up there, riding high with such a great view as the truck wound its way up the narrow, dusty road.

By the time we arrived at the wharf, the ship had already anchored and was in the process of launching a landing craft. In no time, it was coming around the point toward the wharf. The truck was unloaded, each crate and cardboard box carefully placed in the landing craft.

The final item to be placed aboard proved to be the most difficult. Our big Newfoundland dog, King, was apprehensive about climbing down into the boat. Paws braced, King would have remained on the wharf had it not been for the greater strength and determination of Dad and the ship's crew. After wrestling this last item aboard, we were ready to push away from the dock.

As the ship's crew secured the load, we took a few minutes to say goodbye. Many friends and relatives had come to see us off. Grandfather was the last person to kiss me goodbye. I sensed the sadness in his smile. As we passed the end of the wharf, I saw tears streaming down Grandfather's face.

It took only a few minutes to reach the ship. I marvelled at its size, and the high black wall of the ship's hull towering above us. We secured our lifeboat and climbed aboard on a rope ladder (not nearly as difficult as it first appeared). Once on deck, I leaned over the rail and peered down into the small boat containing all our belongings. I saw King looking up at us. It would be interesting, I thought, to see how he was going to get aboard. The rope ladder was clearly not one of his options.

I watched with great excitement as a large boom swung out over the side of the ship. A sling connected to a hook was lowered from the boom into the barge below. The men placed bags and boxes in the sling. A winch hoisted everything straight up. The boom swung back over the ship, and our goods were lowered into the ship's hold. It was not long before everything was loaded.

Everything, that is, except King. I saw two men coaxing him to come and stand on a canvas tarpaulin. When he finally did, they quickly wrapped it around him, forming another sling. He was hoisted up the same way as the cargo. I thought he would surely panic and jump to his death, but he just stood there and peered through the fold in the sling. He was lowered down onto the deck without incident.

Suddenly, thick smoke began pouring from the ship's single funnel. I could see tiny specks of soot, resembling flakes of black snow, falling on the deck and accumulating on the rail. We were leaving. Dad explained that down in the engine room, men were shovelling coal into a stoker hole, fuelling a fire to heat the boilers. The resulting steam would drive the pistons and start the engine. I heard the throb as the cylinders began to beat, slowly at first, then gradually accelerate. The propellers were turning. We were moving forward, pulling away from Neil's Harbour.

I stood on the deck and watched as the small village receded in the wake of the ship. I could see our house, standing there empty and alone, and wondered what would become of it. It took a long time for it to disappear from view, and I stayed there until distance closed the curtain.

As I turned away, I noticed a man in uniform approaching my father. He introduced himself as Captain Talbot. He said we would not be going to St. Paul Island today. A heavy surf (generated by tides and ocean swell) had made landing conditions on the island unsafe. We would spend the night anchored in Aspy Bay, just off Dingwall Harbour. The captain planned to leave for St. Paul Island early in the morning, when the weather there was expected to improve.

The sky was clear and the winds were calm when we dropped anchor in Aspy Bay that evening. The setting sun dipping below the Aspy mountain range painted the sky with brilliant colours. Only the occasional squawk from a passing herring gull interrupted the silence. There was time to sit and reflect on the day's events.

It was unfortunate that my mother and Ina were not here to share the excitement. Dad was leaning over the rail, his eyes fixed on the horizon. I could see that his thoughts were elsewhere. He slowly turned to me and said, "You know, it's a good thing that Ina got sick yesterday and not after we got out to the island. She should be out of surgery by now. Mom will probably send us a message tomorrow." I wondered how and when they would get out to the island now that they had missed the boat.

It was getting chilly when Dad and I left the deck and went inside to our small cabin. When we were both ready for bed, Dad took the lower berth and I climbed into the upper one. The white sheets felt a little cold and damp as I pulled them up over me, but I soon fell asleep in the evening silence.

Next morning I was awakened by the sound of the engine. The steady, rapid pulse of the cylinders indicated that we had been underway for some time. I instantly climbed out of my berth. When I tried to pull on my pants, the ship rolled suddenly. I had to run backwards into

Southwest light station from the water. (Photo by Billy Budge)

the opposite wall in order to remain on my feet. I finished getting dressed and rushed out on the deck to see how far we had come. To my surprise, we were almost there! St. Paul Island was less than a mile away. It was no longer a small hump on the horizon, but a large mass of rocks, cliffs, and trees looming over the ship. Except for two or three small buildings, I could see no sign of human habitation or activity.

As we cruised past the Southwest Point, Dad pointed.

"Billy," he said, "that's our lighthouse up there and just to the right of it is the dwelling house where we will be living."

Silhouetted against the white sky of early morning, the lighthouse stood poised on its rocky promontory, a giant soldier keeping a lonely vigil over the sea. It was unprotected against all of nature's fury. There was not so much as a solitary tree to break the wind. It was now the responsibility of my father to ensure that, bleak and exposed as it was, this light continued to shine, no matter how dark and stormy the night.

Looking up, I could see the dwelling house, slightly below and a short distance to the right of the lighthouse. It was a white, two-storey building with a red roof, sitting upon a steep pasture. The grass behind the house blended into a thick growth of stunted trees. There was no lawn, just a mixture of short, sparse vegetation. In some places there were more rocks than grass. The front yard was even steeper than the back.

From the boat, I could see a fence leading from the house up to the lighthouse. The fence was obviously used by the lighthouse keeper as a handhold and guide while attending to the light on stormy days. Below the fence the steep slope continued down to the water. A short distance below the house, the grass grew thinner, then ended abruptly at the point where a high granite cliff plunged vertically into the ocean.

There were a few other buildings near the house. One appeared to be a small barn and the other, a shed. Beyond that there was nothing I could see except more trees, cliffs, and surf. As our ship slid past the light station, I wondered what my mother would think when she first cast her eyes upon our new home.

A few minutes later the *Lady Laurier* dropped its anchor off Atlantic Cove, about one and a half miles up the coast from our light station. As we prepared to go ashore I noticed a school of dolphins, apparently excited by the noise of the ship, jumping out of the water and putting on quite a performance. Maybe they were the welcoming committee come out to greet us. Who could ask for anything more?

4

A Different World

Going ashore from the *Lady Laurier* could not have been easier. Instead of negotiating the rope ladder as we had coming aboard, the three of us (including King) stepped into one of the lifeboats hanging from the davits, and were lowered into the water. No sooner had we struck the water when the boatsman started the engine. After his helper unhooked the cables from the bow and stern, we were off.

I became a little apprehensive as we approached the cove. Large waves were rolling in and breaking on either side of our small boat. Water is shallow on both sides of Atlantic Cove, and ocean swells curl up and break as they pass over the rocky ledges just beneath the surface. The deeper water in the centre of the channel provides a safe passage into the cove, but the surf generated by these swells sometimes makes it difficult or impossible to land safely on the beach. Our present crew seemed confident that this was not one of those times.

The lifeboat came to a stop slowly, nudging its bow unsteadily against the rocky beach, while its port side brushed against a smooth vertical cliff that towered high over our heads. While the crew held the boat steady we climbed upon the starboard side, and when the waves ceased momentarily, Dad, I and King jumped ashore. We were standing on St. Paul Island at last.

Directly ahead of us was a wooden slip, or boat ramp. It was quite steep, but relatively easy to climb, though use of both hands and feet was required to reach the top. As we stood there in the tall grass and watched the lifeboat heading out to the ship, it was obvious our furniture and supplies would not come ashore the same way.

Fortunately for us, the solution to the problem of getting large items ashore had been solved by some ingenious engineer some years back. Near the edge of the cliff, and directly above where the lifeboat had come in, was a rather large building. Attached to the end of the building was a steel mast from which was suspended a large wooden boom.

I watched with interest as the lifeboat returned with the first load. Once the boat was secured at the base of the cliff, a number of crewmen scrambled up the slip and rushed over to the building. One of them went inside and started the winch engine. With the use of ropes and muscle power, the others swung the boom out over the cliff. A heavy, greasy cable from the winch travelled through a series of pulleys on the ground, ran up the length of the boom and over the last pulley at the end. When the winch operator released the brake, the weight of a heavy steel hook on the end of the cable pulled it down to the crewmen in the boat below.

The first item I saw coming up was our sofa, dangling and spinning high above the water before being pulled in and lowered onto the grass. The rest came ashore in similar fashion, including many bags of coal, barrels of gas and kerosene, and food supplies. Everything, with the exception of the fuel, was placed inside the building. There it would remain until it could be transported up to the Southwest light by means of a farm tractor and wagon.

Dad was expecting the outgoing lighthouse keeper, with the tractor and his family's things (ready to be moved off the island), to be present. However, he was nowhere to be seen. With no other means of transportation available, we decided to head out on foot toward the light station.

The moment we departed the landing area, I could see this was no ordinary road. Our hike began by following wheel imprints in the tall grass leading across the field at the base of Atlantic Cove and into the woods. Just prior to entering the woods, we saw an unusual looking object near the side of the road. It resembled a concrete chair. Dad said it was actually the base of an old sundial. The timepiece itself had long since been removed; only the pedestal was left as a reminder of the island's historic past.

The road through the woods was different. Consisting of two gravel wheel ruts with green vegetation in between, it snaked its way through a dense forest that tightly hemmed it in on either side. Sunlight filtered through the thick canopy. The soil was rather damp, and in some places, tiny streams of water trickled along in the wheel tracks. A short distance up the trail, we came upon a small building with a missing door. The building's interior walls had been destroyed. It was sitting near a concrete dam, built to form a reservoir supplied by water from a tiny stream. At one time, the building had contained a pump to supply water to a military radar site constructed during World War II. It operated from the island's highest elevation at the summit of Mt. Groggan, 485 feet. The site was abandoned when the war ended. After quenching our thirst with a drink of the clear water, we continued up the trail.

The next thing I saw made me stop and rub my eyes in disbelief. A rabbit darted across the road in front of us – a rabbit that was as black as the night! Dad told me these animals were not native to the island. They had been brought here by someone a few years before to see if they would thrive and multiply. Well, we could report that at least one was still alive.

Trees provided shelter for many species of small birds. They appeared to be here in greater abundance than on the mainland. As we walked, I noticed several birds that were unfamiliar to me; my father couldn't identify them either. High overhead, a bald eagle, its massive wings outstretched, soared along in search of prey.

Birds in the trees or in the sky were not the most interesting to my father. More important to Dad were the birds in the water. We could see flocks of various species of seabirds feeding in the surf. An avid duck hunter, Dad intended to hunt these birds for food. Fresh meat would sometimes be in short supply because we would have no refrigerator in which to keep it preserved.

About ten minutes into the hike, we came to a small clearing known as Whistle Point, which had been the site of the first primitive foghorn or steam whistle on St. Paul. It had been abandoned for many years. The only things remaining were an old stone foundation and a portion of the hardwood floor of the dwelling house. An old rusty boiler, once used to generate steam to blow the foghorn, was still clinging to the edge of the cliff.

A few hundred yards further on, the trail meandered along a steep granite incline. The track was barely wide enough to allow the tractor to negotiate the turns. As he looked at the ocean below, Dad expressed concern over the absence of a guardrail at such a treacherous location. This section, known as the "bluff," is the highest elevation on the trail. It offers the greatest perspective, including the entire coastline to the Southwest Point, where one building at the light station was visible. Looking out to sea, we could see the northern section of Cape Breton on the horizon.

Beyond the bluff, the trail returned to its previous character until we came to a swampy area. Here we found ourselves walking across a section of "corduroy road," which consists of small logs lying side by side across the trail. The logs formed a ramp to distribute the weight of the tractor as it travelled over the soft, wet soil. The corduroy was in need of repair. In many places, the tractor had broken through rotten logs, creating deep holes in the mud. No doubt this would be one of the first repair projects that we would have to undertake. After crossing a couple of tiny bridges over trickling streams, we came out of the woods at the Southwest light station. We were home at last.

We passed a series of buildings before arriving at the house. The tractor garage/storage building was the greatest distance from the house; it was the structure that was visible from the bluff. Nearby was a small workshop, and beside that sat the smallest and most important building of all, the outdoor toilet.

The farm tractor was parked near the house, the wagon attached and loaded with the possessions of the outgoing lighthouse keeper. Inside the house, Morris Baker and his wife were enjoying one last cup of coffee. Their two young daughters stood by clutching their dolls, waiting to leave. They offered us something to eat. Dad declined, knowing they were in a hurry to leave and catch the *Lady Laurier*, still anchored off Atlantic Cove. After bidding us good-bye, they hurriedly left. I never saw them again.

It was time to go and check out the house. The back door opened into a long mud room. At the end there were two doorways, one on the left side and another on the right. The room to the left was mostly a storage area; it also held a small generator used to charge the battery for the "radio telephone." The door on the right led into the kitchen, which featured a coal stove for heating and cooking.

In the kitchen, an old-fashioned hand pump was perched on the end of a counter. It pumped water from the cistern beneath the kitchen floor. The cistern, our only water supply, was a concrete tank that collected and stored rainwater that ran off the roof. Hot water was available only if you remembered to fill the copper tank on the back of the stove and kept the fire going. A pantry located to the right of the kitchen provided the only cupboard space in the whole house.

From the kitchen, a doorway led into the living room. It was empty except for the radio telephone that would provide us with our only communication to the mainland. A marine radio station in North Sydney called twice a day, to confirm everything was in order at the light station. This was also Dad's opportunity to send and receive messages. The operators at the radio station told us that they monitored the frequency at all times, in case of an emergency. We would later discover that this was not true.

There was nothing unusual about the four bedrooms upstairs, except for the windows. Each window in every bedroom offered a spectacular view. One could look out over the cliffs, the ocean, or the lighthouse and study the ships cruising past the island. After I decided which bedroom I wanted, we left the house and headed back to the landing to get the tractor.

The landing was deserted by the time we arrived and the *Lady Laurier* was gone. The farm tractor, parked next to the building, was finally ours. We began to load the wagon with those items necessary to make the first night as comfortable as possible. The only things we needed were a couple of beds, a table and chairs and, of course, something to eat.

We were just about to climb up on the tractor when Dad noticed a gentleman coming toward us from the dwelling house above the cove. Introducing himself as Stan Cairns, the radio operator at Atlantic Cove, he invited us up to his house for coffee. This time Dad accepted the offer. It was the third time that day I had been deprived of a ride on the tractor and I was quite disappointed.

At Mr. Cairn's house we met his wife, Ruth, who prepared a snack for which I was very grateful. I had not eaten since early morning. I also met their four-year-old son, Martin, who was only two when he came to St. Paul Island. Later Mr. Cairns took us up to the wireless station. I watched with great excitement as he tapped out messages using Morse code.

We left the wireless station in late afternoon, and once again headed for our tractor. There could be no more delays: the lighthouse was our responsibility, and it would have to be in operation by sunset. My father gave me some room on the tractor seat with him and we headed up the trail. It was "steady as she goes," motoring along in the fresh air with our wagonload of supplies until we reached "the bluff." Here Dad stopped the tractor and said, "Billy, you step off and walk behind the tractor until we get past this section." Once we were safely around the bluff, I got back up with Dad. Shortly afterwards we arrived at the lighthouse.

Lengthening shadows reminded us that the sun would soon be setting. The lighthouse would need our immediate attention. Our lighthouse was a thirty-foot high steel cylinder – height was not necessary at the top of a cliff. A steel ladder just inside the door allowed the keeper to reach the light assembly on the upper floor.

Activating the light in the lighthouse was a complicated procedure. First, it was necessary to carry containers of kerosene up the ladder and then pour the fuel into a tank. Another tank had to be manually pumped up with air to a specified pressure. Weights had to be winched up, mantels replaced, generator tubes cleaned, and all the lenses and prisms polished. Sometimes, it would take almost an hour just to light the light. Then it required a constant watch throughout the night to en-

sure that it remained operational. I watched with interest as Dad completed
the various steps of preparation. Finally, with the
strike of a match, the light
was lit and burning brightly. We then left for the
house, where my father
made his first entry into
the station log book: "12
September, 1955; Time of
lighting: 1820 DST;
Weather: Sunny."

Later we unloaded the
furniture from the wagon
and temporarily set up
housekeeping. In one of
the boxes Dad found a
piece of bologna and a
package of doughnuts,
which we scoffed down
before calling it a day. I

The Southwest Lighthouse in the 1950s.
Eventually the lighthouse was removed and
reassembled as an ornament in the parking
lot of the Canadian Coast Guard station in
Dartmouth, Nova Scotia. (Photo by Edith
Budge)

dozed off on the living room floor, the rotating lenses in the lighthouse
casting strange shadows and weird shapes on the walls. Next morning
when I awoke, Dad had breakfast ready and on the table. The special
that morning was bread and butter served with ketchup and bologna.
We needed a hearty breakfast before facing another strenuous day of
hauling our supplies to the light station.

Before we began the day's work, Dad turned on the radio telephone
for the morning schedule. At the appointed time we received the following transmission: "This is VCO North Sydney Radio to all lighthouses.
We have one message today for Southwest St. Paul."

After they called each lighthouse individually and received a response, they called us and read the message. It was from my mother,
telling us Ina was recovering from surgery and would be out of the hos-

pital soon. Meanwhile, arrangements were being made with a fishing boat for their transportation out to the island. This good news eased our minds and we were better able to concentrate on hauling supplies and preparing the house for Mom's arrival. The operation seemed to move more quickly now, and by noontime all the furniture had been hauled up and arranged inside the house. Again we dined on bologna sandwiches, then continued with the chores and fetching the groceries.

There was enough food waiting for us inside the shed at the landing to set up a market. There were cases of canned milk, meat and beans, plus everything else you would find on the shelf of a grocery store. There were large bags of potatoes, carrots and other vegetables. Boxes of dry food products were spread over the floor and with the exception of fresh meat, there were enough groceries to last our family a year. Dad had another idea for fresh meat, although there was some risk involved in its preservation. He believed that if fresh meat were delivered in December, the average outside air temperature would keep it frozen all winter.

Each year as the shipping season drew to a close in the Gulf of St. Lawrence, a Department of Transport supply ship would make its final run. The purpose of this voyage was to remove all buoys, markers, and other aids to navigation that might otherwise be damaged or destroyed by the moving ice floes. Usually this was done during the latter part of December. Even though the supply ship was not required to deliver supplies to the lighthouses on this trip, they made a practice of dropping off fresh meat and other last-minute items that lighthouse keepers needed for winter. They would also bring along the mail, and perhaps one or two Christmas parcels.

We looked forward to the arrival of this ship with great apprehension because there was a catch. If the weather conditions were unfavourable and a safe landing was not possible, the ship did not wait for the situation to improve. We referred to this boat as the Christmas boat, but because of its unreliability Santa Claus could hardly depend on it for transportation. Therefore, our parents did their Christmas shopping earlier by mail. This guaranteed arrival on the September supply ship.

Over the course of the next few days we hauled the remainder of the foodstuffs, as well as various parts and equipment for the lighthouse, to the Southwest light. I helped my father roll the barrels of kerosene and gas up wooden planks and into the wagon. At the light station we rolled them into the fuel shed, where Dad stood them on end and properly positioned them. Coal, the only item remaining, was the most difficult. I grew to despise it; the bags were dirty and awkward to handle. Yet, even at the age of seven, I could help with this work, and my father was impressed with my ef-

Dad, me and Ina with Prince on our customized tractor with the rear seat. (Photo by Edith Budge)

forts. Although they were heavy, I could lift the bags at about my waist height off the pile and carry them over to the wagon. Once Dad had them safely stacked on board we were off with another load.

As we proceeded up a long grade with the first load of coal, I heard a thump under the tractor. When I turned around I saw the wagon-load of coal heading down the hill from us. It rolled up a steep bank and into some small trees before coming to a stop. Fortunately, it did not overturn nor sustain any damage. We had to unload all that miserable coal before we could get the wagon back on the road. We later discovered that a rock in the centre of the road had knocked out the hitch pin, disconnecting the trailer. Dad had mentioned fixing a seat in the wagon for Mom and Ina, but after this mishap he realized that riding in the wagon was dangerous. Furthermore, it was inconvenient to tow around. There had to be a better way.

As soon as the last bag of coal was hauled, and before Mom and Ina arrived, Dad came up with a solution. He selected a number of boards from a small pile of lumber near the workshop and began to construct a large box. When it was completed we attached it to the three-point-hitch on the back of the tractor with brackets and U-bolts. After a bench was installed across the back of the box, we had the only farm tractor in Cape Breton with a rear seat. This new addition featured full legroom, seating capacity for three, and a backrest. I was pleased with the job we had done. I was sure Mom would be proud to ride in such comfort and style.

On the evening of September 23rd we received another message on the radio telephone. It stated that, weather permitting, Mom and Ina would be arriving on a fishing boat the next day. The timing was right as my taste for bologna was beginning to wane and I longed for a home-cooked meal. Dad said that we would celebrate this joyous occasion with our first hot dinner since we arrived on the island. Later that evening, by the flickering light of an oil lamp, we sat down to enjoy a meal of boiled potatoes, carrots, onions, and – you guessed it – fried bologna!

Next morning we arose early as we had much work to do before Mom arrived at our new home. An untidy house would be unacceptable to Mother. Dad swept the floor and I tidied up, all the while watching the horizon for an approaching fishing boat. Later that morning, Dad noticed a small speck in the distance coming toward the island. In order to arrive at the landing in time, we left at once on our tractor to meet them.

As soon as the boat anchored in the cove, Mom and Ina climbed into a small rowboat and one of the fisherman rowed them into the landing. As they approached the beach I anxiously waited to hug my mother and tell her all about St. Paul Island. Yet even from a distance the absence of a single smile indicated that she did not share my excitement about our new home. Ina, because of her age, showed no emotion at all. I couldn't wait to tell her about all the things I had discovered on the island and all the places left to explore. Dad helped them ashore and led them over the slippery rocks.

Watching them climb up the cliff, I noticed how well they were dressed (although not suitable for the occasion). Ina was dressed in a dark skirt with white leotards and shiny black shoes, her long blond hair neatly combed. I had often watched Mom take small sections of Ina's hair in her hand, comb it tightly around her finger and then let it go.

When completed her hair hung down in a series of long ringlets that bounced like miniature slinky toys when she ran. My mother wore a light-coloured skirt and a hand-knitted wool sweater. Her dark brown hair was partially covered by a silk bandanna tied under her chin. Mom had some difficulty climbing the ramp, but soon they both reached the safety of the grass. The long boat ride, as well as a slight case of sea-sickness, caused her limp to be more pronounced as she walked across the field. When we reached the tractor I was anxious to ask Mom what she thought about St. Paul Island now that she was finally here. I never asked the question: the answer was written on her face, and it was obvious she was not impressed. Sensing her disappointment and trying to cheer her up, I said, "You won't believe this place, Mom. It's wonderful."

There was one more item to come ashore before we left the landing. My mother believed that no matter where we lived it was important to have clean clothes, so with that in mind she had brought along a wringer washing machine. She traded in her new electric model for a gas-engine powered model. It was similar to her electric wringer washer, except this one had a small, greasy engine attached conspicuously to the base. Using the winch and boom, we hoisted up the washing machine and placed it in the shed.

With Mom and Ina perched up in the new back seat, and myself sharing the main seat with Dad, we cruised along in "Beverly Hillbilly" style. Dad stopped at the bluff for Mom to take in the view. He pointed out the fishing boat, now on its way back to the mainland. My mother's only response was, "Freddy, do you suppose there's still enough time for me to catch that boat?"

It took only a few days for my mother to begin feeling more comfortable with living on St. Paul Island. Ruth and Stan Cairns came to visit now and then, and I'm sure this helped Mom adjust to the isolation. Even though the Cairns were becoming good friends, Mom recognized the need to be independent. The wireless station at Governor's Cove was due to close the following summer, and nobody would be replacing the Cairns family.

Mom became familiar with her household environment and learned to adapt to a lifestyle more consistent with earlier times. We in-

stalled the washing machine in the storeroom beside the small generator. Mom seemed to love using that noisy monster, unaware that sometime in the near future it would twice almost succeed in taking her life.

Dad and I spent time improving living conditions outside the
house. We repaired the worst places in the road by filling in the holes
and flattening the bumps. With a fair amount of difficulty we even built
a fence around the bluff. It was primitively constructed but strong
enough to prevent the tractor from taking its occupants on a fatal ride
should a wheel suddenly slip over the edge of the road.

By the time Dad and I had finished all the necessary repairs around
the station, it was well into October and time to open the schoolbooks.
Even though we were more than a month late beginning school work,
Dad wanted all lessons up to date by December. They were to be ready
to mail out on the elusive Christmas boat.

The teacher's guide defined what lessons were to be completed, and
often included a brief illustration showing proper procedure for the exercise. It also made clear which lessons were to be completed in our
notebook, and what was to be done on special paper and mailed to Halifax for correction. My parents worked out a schedule for school: classes
were to be conducted in the afternoon and evening hours, Monday
through Friday. At first Ina and I did our studies on opposite ends of the
dining room table; later I would build a desk for each of us. During the
evening hours we studied under the dim light of an Aladdin lamp.
Time was not important to us. Even though the guide was designed to
correspond with calender dates, we soon discovered that by keeping a
steady pace and working a few extra hours, we could often complete a
regular school week in just three days.

Mornings were best for duck hunting, and this time of day was re-
served for that activity. Each morning, I would tag along behind my father, walking the coastline looking for any seabirds close enough to the
shore to shoot. My father carried a 12-gauge shotgun; I had to settle for
a lowly air rifle. No matter how close we got to a duck (and it was never
very close), my air rifle was totally useless for killing any kind of sea-
bird. I was so unhappy with this gun that Dad promised to buy me a .22
calibre rifle at the first opportunity.

Meanwhile, Father was having duck troubles of his own. He was sure that King, who loved to swim, would make an excellent retriever. He was wrong. With a little persuasion, King would swim out to the dead birds, look them over and then swim back to shore without them. King would gladly repeat the trip, but would not take the birds into his mouth no matter how much Dad yelled, swore or pleaded.

On St. Paul Island, necessity became the mother of invention. Dad cut down a slender tree and snipped off the branches. He then bent the tree into a large hoop, and attached a small portion of large mesh netting to the inside. Finally, he took a length of heavy fishing line and bridled it to the hoop. He had created a large dip net on a lanyard. From then on, Dad would go off hunting with his shotgun over his shoulder and the hula-hoop retriever on his back. It might take several attempts, but he was usually successful in tossing this device out over the dead birds and then pulling them into the net and onto the shore.

With most of our problems resolved, and Christmas only a few weeks away, it should have been a time to be joyous. On a chilly afternoon in mid-December, while splitting kindling, I lifted my head and saw a tall stranger standing over me.

"Hi," he said. "My name is George, and I've walked up from the Northeast."

When I introduced myself he asked, "Is your father around? I'd like to speak to him."

5

Tragedy on the Northeast

Our visitor's name was George Gatza. George had come to St. Paul Island in 1953 to serve as assistant lighthouse keeper at the Northeast. He applied for the job on St. Paul Island while he was lighthouse keeper at Low Point, near Sydney, Nova Scotia. After being awarded the position on St. Paul, he and his wife, Mary, moved to the island. They took up residence in one of the dwellings on the Northeast. That cold December day when I first met George, he was well-seasoned in the ways of lighthouse life, with two years of experience living on an island. Still, he seemed ill at ease. He kept shifting his weight from one foot to the other as he stood there talking to me, unable to relax. Tall and muscular, he spoke with a soft voice in mellow tones.

Inside our house, he shared his concerns with my parents. This Christmas meant more to George than had those of previous years: he and his wife were expecting their first child. Mary was six months along in her pregnancy. George had planned on giving her a surprise, and was anxiously awaiting the arrival of a couple of parcels on the December supply ship. He was worried as he was aware of the policy of the December boat not waiting around for good weather. The supply ship *Edward Cornwallis* was already en route from Halifax to Sydney, where it would pick up those last-minute items for the lighthouses, including George's two coveted parcels. I could share his excitement since a new .22 calibre rifle Dad had ordered for me was due to arrive on the same boat.

Mary and George Gatza

Before he left our house to return to the Northeast, he paused for a moment on the doorstep and looked toward the mainland. Although the weather was overcast, the ocean was calm. The water below the lighthouse stirred only slightly among the rocks.

"If only the supply ship were here today," George said to my mother, "they could land supplies anywhere on the island."

He then bade us goodbye, with the hope that the current weather would hold until the ship arrived. Dad insisted that George accept a ride on the tractor as far as the landing, leaving him only half the distance to walk. George agreed to the ride with some reluctance, since he had come to the Southwest for a hike and some friendly conversation. Dad let him off at the end of the road near the wireless station. At this point there was only a footpath leading to the Northeast. George followed this difficult trail as far as the tittle, where he climbed into the boatswain chair and pulled himself across the channel to his home on the Northeast.

On the morning of 20 December, Mom woke me with much excitement in her voice. "Billy," she said, "the supply ship *Edward Cornwallis* is anchored off Atlantic Cove now, and your father has already left for the landing."

Earlier she had heard the ship's captain talking on the radio telephone, saying he felt conditions were favourable enough to land what

The Northeast, off the northern tip of St. Paul Island showing the tittle or narrow channel. (Photo by Billy Budge)

few supplies they had that day. I scrambled quickly out of bed and rushed to my bedroom window, only to find I could not see anything outside – my window was covered with thick frost.

I blew on one of the panes to soften the heavy accumulation and scraped a small section clear with my fingernails. Sure enough, Mom was right. I could even see a small craft leaving the ship and heading in toward shore.

While we were eating breakfast, the radio telephone crackled in the corner, interrupted now and again by sporadic bursts of ship-to-shore conversation. We listened to every word, making sure that everything was going well. Mom was anxiously awaiting the arrival of the mail. She hoped for a letter from Grandfather, as well as cards and messages from other relatives and friends back home. Even though it was only five days until Christmas, Ina was sure that Grandfather had sent her some small item to be enjoyed immediately. I was looking forward to doing some serious duck hunting with that new rifle (after a few lessons from Dad about proper use and safety when handling such a dangerous weapon). There would also be outgoing mail, including a large brown envelope containing the lessons Ina and I had been required to complete to date. We had been so diligent in our schoolwork that some January assignments were also enclosed.

According to the radio conversation, there were going to be problems landing on the Northeast. A gale-force wind had been blowing out of the northwest for several days. The windward side of St. Paul Island was being pounded by heavy surf. Atlantic Cove, on the lee side, had almost no wave action at all. The problem at the Northeast was in the tittle, that narrow channel between the two islands. The channel is aligned in an east-west direction and the northwest wind was funnelling the waves straight through the passage. The force of these waves, combined with the tidal flow, had turned the waters of the channel into a boiling cauldron. On the Northeast, the tittle was the only place to land.

Their landing was different from ours at Atlantic Cove. Although they had a winch as we had, there was no boom to hoist up the supplies. A ramp or boardwalk extended from the lighthouse down to the water's edge at the tittle. The landing barge would tie up at the end of the ramp and unload its cargo. On one side of the ramp a miniature rail car attached to a cable rolled along on a set of narrow steel tracks. The heavier items such as barrels of fuel were placed on this carriage, and were then winched a couple of hundred yards up to the lighthouse.

Based on radio conversation between the captain of the *Edward Cornwallis* and Joe Mitchell, the lighthouse keeper on the Northeast, it appeared that George Gatza's worst fears would be realized. The captain stated that he would not attempt to make a landing on the Northeast due to heavy sea in the channel. Once the landing at Atlantic Cove was completed, the ship would leave the island. George must have felt that his packages were too large or heavy to carry on his back over the difficult trail from the Atlantic Cove landing to the Northeast, otherwise Dad could have accepted them.

A short time later, however, the captain agreed to a possible solution to the dilemma on the Northeast. He suggested that if a suitable site could be found on the main island near the Northeast, they would make an attempt to land there. Immediately George left in search of some small cove or crevice in the rocks where the water was calm enough to toss those few parcels ashore.

George persuaded Merlyn Baker, one of the other assistants, to accompany him. They each donned some extra clothing and rushed down to the boatswain chair. Before pulling oneself across the tittle, it was necessary to put on a pair of heavy protective gloves. Over the years, the cable had been continually subjected to wind and salt spray. It had never received any kind of maintenance. The gloves were necessary to protect one's hands from broken strands of steel that protruded from the cable like rusty needles.

As the two men climbed into the chair, neither of them noticed a more serious problem. Severe corrosion had taken place where the pulleys of the chair were left siting on the cable when it was not in use. This corrosion had taken place over a long period of time; it is easy to understand why a frequent user may not have noticed such gradual deterioration. A few minutes later they pulled themselves away from the shore in a chair that would never reach the other side.

They had barely reached mid-span when, without warning, the cable snapped. The chair dropped into the channel, tossing the two men into the frigid water. Merlyn lost consciousness for one or two seconds from the shock of the sudden cold. When he revived, he saw a large wave rolling toward him. In a moment it engulfed him, and swept him along with such force that he was at the mercy of the sea. When the wave subsided he found himself on a ledge of rock partly out of the water. He scrambled the rest of the way up the cliff to safety.

Merlyn turned around and saw that there had been no lucky wave for his friend. George appeared to be swimming erratically while the strong current was sweeping him out the channel toward the open sea. Merlyn called out to him in the hope that the sound of his voice would give him some sense of direction. George did not respond, and Merlyn noticed that he had also stopped swimming. Although he knew it was already too late, Merlyn searched for a piece of rope that he could throw out to George. Nearby he found a small coil lying on the rocks. When he touched the coil he realized it was useless: it had been left out in the weather and was frozen in a solid mass.

When Merlyn looked up again, George had been swept away. He was only thirty years old. Merlyn ran with the news of the tragedy to the lighthouse keeper, who placed a frantic call to the captain of the *Edward*

Cornwallis, still anchored off Atlantic Cove. In minutes the ship weighed anchor and was en route to the Northeast. The crew spent the remainder of the day searching the area in hope that George may have survived, though they knew no one could live long in the frigid water of late December. By nightfall the search was abandoned. George's body was never recovered.

Later that day, the *Edward Cornwallis*'s crew was successful in landing the packages for the Northeast. This was accomplished by using a series of ropes attached between the lifeboat and the shore. The parcels were pulled ashore on the ropes – the same parcels that had cost George his life.

The captain relayed a radio message to George's widow, Mary, offering his condolences. He also apologized for being unable to take her off the island. However, he may have been a little insensitive when he asked if she could wait until after Christmas to be airlifted off. It was somewhat cruel to even suggest waiting on a remote island to an expectant mother grieving the loss of her husband at Christmastime. She was there alone without any family or friends to comfort her. Obviously, she had not grasped the magnitude of the situation since she agreed to wait until after Christmas.

The next day, however, she was seized by the grim reality of her circumstances and required immediate medical attention. A radio call for assistance was sent, and a Navy helicopter was dispatched from Halifax. The strong wind caused much concern when the helicopter arrived at the Northeast. There were a few anxious moments before it finally touched down. Mary was placed aboard and flown to Sydney. Three months later, she delivered a baby boy whom she called George, after his late father.

6

The First Winter

It was only a few days before Christmas. Ina and I were as excited as kids everywhere at that time of year. Ina was too young to comprehend what had just happened on the Northeast, and I soon forgot it. My parents appeared to be filled with the spirit of the season, though the recent tragedy must have weighed heavily on their minds. Their hearts ached for Mrs. Gatza, who would endure her grief through this time of year. There would not even be a funeral to provide a closure to her husband's life. With the attitude that life must go on, my parents put the matter to rest and began to prepare for Christmas.

Two days before Christmas, Dad picked up the axe and I followed him down the trail toward the landing in search of a suitable tree. It was easy to find a Christmas tree on St. Paul Island: small fir trees grew in abundance. Selecting one with the proper shape from the dense clusters of new growth was a little more difficult. Eventually, we returned home with a tree that made my mother proud. This would be our first Christmas on the island, and the only Christmas we would enjoy the company of neighbours from the wireless station at Atlantic Cove.

Decorating was done according to family tradition. Dad put up the tree the afternoon of Christmas Eve, and Mom trimmed it in the evening. Ina and I were both anxious to help, but I sensed that Mother would rather be left alone. Often she would hold an ornament in her hand for the longest time before placing it on the tree. The decorations seemed to speak to her in distant voices, echoing through time from Christmases past. Many were gifts from friends or relatives whom she would not see this year. She wondered where they were now; if only they could drop by for tea. This is the only time I recall noticing my mother's loneliness.

While my mother, wistfully remembering livelier times, finished decorating the tree, Dad looked for something to brighten the spirit. He tuned the radio to CJCB in Sydney, where the DJ was playing Christmas music all the time. When we knew the words, we all joined in with the songs on the radio. The singing seemed to bring us together. We helped Mother place the last few bells on the tree, and went to bed to await the arrival of Santa Claus.

Christmas morning of 1955 arrived with all of nature's fury. Snow had begun falling during the night. The wind had come up, and by dawn had hit gale force. Howling wind swept over and around our unsheltered home, making an eerie sound more reminiscent of Halloween than Christmas. The snow had so reduced the visibility that we could barely see the ocean below the cliff. Little snow was accumulating on the ground: the wind was sweeping it horizontally past the station and out to sea. This was the first snowstorm of the winter, and a taste of things to come.

Ina and I cared little about the weather outside. It was Christmas, and time to check under the tree. Maybe, we worried, the weather was a little too much for old St. Nick. There was the chance that he missed our house, standing alone on this rock in the ocean.

Our fears were unfounded. Mom had made certain that Christmas on St. Paul Island would be no different than anywhere else. We opened our gifts with the excitement of kids everywhere. Soon the wrappings and gifts were strewn all over the floor. With great appreciation for what we had received, we helped Mom clean up the mess. Then everyone went to breakfast.

The gift that I had looked forward to receiving the most turned out to be a major disappointment. I had asked my parents for "Meccano," an erector set containing numerous strips of pre-drilled metal and scores of nuts and bolts to build various projects. When my mother ordered the set she noticed that they were numbered in series all the way up to ten. She ordered set Number One, thinking she was making the correct decision. When I attempted to build one of the projects in the book, half the necessary parts were not there. It was then that we noticed that I required the previous set, Number Zero, without which none of the projects could be completed. After I drooled over the book containing all those fine machines that I couldn't build, Mom put it away until the missing set could be acquired.

Boxing Day dawned bright and sunny. We rushed outside to see how much snow had fallen. Dad took the tractor out of the garage, and decided that we would all go down to the wireless station and visit with the Cairns. The snow was quite deep on portions of the trail, causing the tractor to spin its wheels while climbing some of the steeper hills.

The view from the bluff was spectacular. Fresh-fallen snow had drifted in swirls around the large boulders and formed gentle slopes against the low trees. A continuous white sheet covered the sparse vegetation of the slope stretching beneath us, extending all the way to the ocean. Only the granite rocks at the water's edge were bare, the restless surf having licked away the snow there. The sky was a brilliant blue and the sun's rays danced across a glistening silver sea. The whiteness of the distant mountains on the mainland gave proof that the people of northern Cape Breton had shared our snowstorm. This magnificent scene from God's own hand was for our eyes only.

The remainder of the trail was generally downhill and we had little trouble reaching the wireless station. Dad walked up to the radio site to chat with Stan Cairns while the rest of us visited at the residence. It was there I met Earl O'Halloran, the other radio operator. Earl was serving his second year of duty on St. Paul Island. He was also a ham radio operator. I watched with interest as Earl, seated in a small room full of equipment, tuned the dials on a panel. He was speaking into a microphone and ending each transmission with the words, "This is VE1-

KG." Although on a remote island, he could talk to other amateur radio operators around the world.

Earl also enjoyed wood carving, and his handiwork was scattered around the room. Whittling helped him pass the time, providing relaxation and enjoyment. One carving in particular caught my eye. It was a Buckingham Palace guard that stood about two feet high. The sentry was actually an ashtray stand, with the ashtray placed in the

In the show at Whistle Point with King. (Photo by Edith Budge)

guard's held-out hand. It was vividly painted with the bright red and black colours of the guard, including the stripe in the pants. I was so impressed with this project that I was determined to try to carve one myself.

Our visit with the neighbours at Atlantic Cove ended early that afternoon. My father was concerned about the road conditions and the possibility of having to shovel should the tractor become stuck. Although there were no problems returning home, it was obvious to everyone that soon the farm tractor would be of little use for winter transportation. It was not equipped with a snowplough. Dad motored down to the landing a couple more times over the next few days. On the final trip he brought the Cairns up for a visit. After that, the continuous accumulation of snow ended any further use of the tractor until spring.

When the next snowstorm came on January 9th, another form of transportation had to be found. When we tried walking after the storm, Dad found it difficult and I found it nearly impossible. For some reason he had forgotten to bring his snowshoes to the island. He felt it would be simple enough to make a primitive pair of snowshoes, and immediately began working on this new project. He found an old piece of weathered plywood that had been left outside, and carved out oval shapes about the size of snowshoes. After giving careful consideration to weight and balance, he attached bootstraps at just the right location. He then laced them to his feet and headed out into the snow for a trial run.

He had made only a few steps into the deep snow when a major flaw in the design became apparent. With each footstep, the snowshoe slid deeply into the snow. Only with great exertion could it be lifted up, bearing a heaping load of snow. When he tried to stand gently on top of the snow, the snowshoe slipped to the left or right, causing him to slide sideways down the grade. Any attempt to move forward caused him to trip and fall as the flat toe of the shoe dug deep into the snow. Dad was not impressed with the test results, but Mom found it most amusing. Finally, he conceded that the only way he could get around with these snowshoes was to carry them under his arm. There would be no patent pending for this latest invention.

A few days later, a call was received on the radio telephone that prompted my father to make a more concerted effort to resolve the transportation problem. The captain of the *Lady Laurier* called from North Sydney. He told us his ship would sail past the island within the next few days, and asked my father if there was anything that he needed. If the weather conditions were favourable, they could drop things off at the landing. Dad took advantage of this surprise visit and placed an order. The short list included a couple of small household items, several pounds of fresh meat, as well as a few dozen eggs. The whole order could be placed in one or two boxes and somehow we would find a way to bring it home from the landing.

We could still walk to the landing, but with difficulty. Returning the one and a half miles carrying a couple boxes of groceries would be nearly impossible. Almost immediately another construction project was in the works. King would be the driving force behind this one. Pulling a sleigh was one thing that King could do well. Dad had used him extensively in Neil's Harbour hauling firewood out of the woods. He had brought along his harness when we moved to St. Paul, but he did not bring the sleigh.

In the workshop near the house, the missing component was rapidly taking shape. From selected pieces of stock I watched my father form the sleigh piece by piece. First, he installed the rails and the bunks and set things up to receive the runners. These he fashioned out of hardwood planks we found on a beach. He bent them into place by pouring buckets of boiling water over the section to be curved. The hot water and steam made the runners easier to bend, and kept the wood from breaking. It was a fine looking sleigh when he pulled it outside (and seemed to have far more potential than the snowshoes).

The morning we heard the news that the *Lady Laurier* was departing North Sydney, Dad harnessed the dog and attached him to the sleigh. We left immediately for the landing, Dad and King leading the way, and me following in their footsteps. The sleigh slid gracefully over the snow while I plodded along, struggling to keep pace. I wanted to sit on the sleigh and enjoy the ride, but Dad reminded me that King would need his strength for the return trip.

With a good distance yet to cover before reaching the landing, I was beginning to feel tired. It was then that I noticed, for a short distance ahead of us, there was bare ground. Water trickling along the wheel ruts had melted the snow and provided me the pleasure of easy walking for a few yards. It felt so relaxing to walk on the bare ground that I wished my father would leave me there to walk back and forth until he returned. I never shared this thought with my father; it would reveal my weakness and I was determined not to fail. Those last few easy steps served to renew my strength. I stepped forward proudly into the deep snow once again, and we soon reached the reservoir. From there the walking was easy, as the trail was downhill the rest of the way. Our timing worked well: we arrived at the landing just as the ship was dropping anchor off the cove.

There was no need to fire up the winch or swing out the boom for such a small delivery. We met the lifeboat on the beach, where they tossed ashore three small cardboard boxes and a bag of mail. They were soon secured to the sleigh and once again we found ourselves mushing up the trail. Somehow, the walk seemed less taxing on the return. Following at the rear, I enjoyed a trail that had become a well-beaten path made by three previous sets of footprints. It would have been much better had King not chosen to make his own trail. Those fresh eggs, so carefully secured on the sleigh, would be a welcome treat. The thought of fried ham and eggs seemed to spur me on. We were making good progress, and I marvelled at how effortlessly King was hauling this load.

Only moments after we passed the bluff our luck changed – things just went to the dogs. A black rabbit jumped out on the trail and sped up the path ahead of us. King, keen for the chase, suddenly developed an appetite for rabbit. He wanted this fellow for lunch. Snow sprayed from all four paws as he developed maximum thrust. Soon both he and the sleigh were flying close behind the rabbit. In a tactical manoeuvre, the rabbit veered left and darted down over the edge of the road into the bushes. In hot pursuit, King also departed the trail, continuing the chase down the slope. Suddenly, the sleigh collided with a low bush and slid halfway up a tree. The sudden stop of the overturned sleigh ejected the parcels into the snow. Partially suspended in midair by his harness, King continued to bark at the rabbit as it disappeared into the bushes. My father's failure to see the humour in all of this only added to the chaos. We quickly cleaned things up at the scene of the accident and resumed the hike. King was not successful in his attempt to catch the rabbit, but he made a fine mess of scrambled eggs!

I arrived home that day just in time for school. It was already afternoon and the beginning of another school day. Working alone with correspondence studies affords one the privilege of progressing at his or her own pace. Quite often, when I found myself ahead of schedule, Dad would declare an unexpected holiday, thus allowing us to hunt the entire day. A holiday, however, did not excuse us from the evening class.

Ina's thinking during class was influenced more by the world immediately around her than by what she was taught in the textbooks. On one occasion, my mother read her a nature lesson in which the intent was to teach children about the life cycle of small birds. The story told of how the birds came northward in the spring, built nests in the trees, raised their young, and then flew south for the winter. At the end of the text a question was asked: "Where do the birds go for the winter?" Ina was familiar with the way Dad and I constantly hunted ducks and kept a daily lookout for new flocks on the ocean. Her reply came swiftly –

"That's a silly question, Mom. Everybody knows that they all go out in the water for the winter!"

With my new .22 calibre rifle, I was much more enthused about duck hunting. When we were within shooting range of a flock, I now had a powerful gun. The actual bagging of a prize would be entirely dependent on how well I aimed. My first kill came about as a result of luck, not from my skill as a marksman. During our time on St. Paul we rarely shot ducks in flight. They seldom, if ever, flew close enough to shore to place themselves within gunshot range. The ducks would usually land in the water some distance from shore, then swim in near the cliffs to feed on sea urchins in the shallows. We would have to guess where they would choose to feed, and be there waiting.

Quite often this plan didn't work, as it didn't on my lucky day. We had grown tired of waiting for ducks that never came. I had been sitting quietly for a long time behind an icy rock that served as a blind and was shivering in the bitter cold. Just as we were about to leave, Dad noticed a lone duck flying close off the point. It was a long shot, but Dad suggested I give it a try. My .22 rifle had a longer range than his 12- gauge shotgun. With arms shaking from the cold, I held up the gun, took aim, and squeezed the trigger. To my surprise, the bird fell from the air and struck the water. However, it was still alive. Resting my gun on a slippery rock, I took careful aim, fired again, and killed it. When the wind blew the dead bird close to the shore, Dad pulled it in with his hoop retriever. The following Sunday, my mother cooked it for dinner and somehow it tasted better than any before.

Around the latter part of January, the drift ice arrived. Carried down from the upper regions of the Gulf of St. Lawrence by wind and tide, it completely surrounded the island in only a few days. It first arrived in small clumps resembling slush on the water. This early ice is called slob ice. It would take only a few more days for larger pans to appear. Before long, some of those individual sheets of ice would cover vast areas of the ocean.

Drift ice was not something new to me, having lived in Neil's Harbour, but here on St. Paul Island it had a different character. In Neil's Harbour, the wind would move the fields of drift ice gently against the shore, where it remained for a few days. When the wind changed direction it would silently drift out to sea again. In this fashion the ice would come and go all winter, until one day in the spring it went out and never came back.

On St. Paul Island, the drift ice was neither gentle nor silent. The island sits in the Cabot Strait like a rock in a stream, resisting both the flow of water and the movement of ice. Because it lies crosswise to the flow, great turbulence develops at the ends. We saw the action from the southwest end.

We would often sit beside the kitchen window and watch the flow of ice slipping past the station. It could reach speeds of up to four or five knots an hour, as if in a rush to cover the last few miles to the open Atlantic. We could see the ice slide over and around Paddy's Rock, a small rock about three hundred feet from shore. The ice made strange growling sounds, as though annoyed by the rock's presence, which slowed its progress only a little.

At other times, the drift ice remained motionless against the shore. The lack of movement caused even greater disturbance. Tremendous forces acted upon the ice trapped against the island, at first causing only loud creaking and groaning noises. When tide pressure reached a certain point, the outside pans of ice would suddenly rise up and, with much tearing and scraping, slide over the sheets next to the shore. The following sheet could not slide over the first two, and had to withstand the pressure until it too began to bow upwards. Finally, with an explosive sound and a shower of ice fragments, it snapped. Broken ice was deposited over the foremost sheets. A wall of ice made of broken and shattered pans quickly formed along the shore. At night, falling asleep to the eerie sounds and continuous explosions of the restless ice took some getting used to.

The St. Lawrence Seaway was closed to shipping after the winter freeze-up, but there were still ships attempting to navigate the Gulf. In the spring, when drift ice conditions were most severe, the seal hunt got underway. The sealing boats cruised west past St. Paul, on their way to intercept the herds of newborn Harp seals on the ice in the central portion of the Gulf of St. Lawrence. Heavy ice created problems for these ships. Quite often in the morning we would observe a ship sailing west apparently making good progress through the ice. In the afternoon, however, that same ship could be seen further east, having lost considerable ground to the force of the moving ice field. When my father tuned his short wave radio receiver to the marine band, we would hear the frustrated captain telling someone about how many miles he had lost during the course of the day. Perhaps pushing some of these ships out of the Gulf was nature's way of protecting the seal herd.

The morning we woke to find the drift ice finally gone, something more sinister had replaced it. We were in the midst of an invasion by the foreign fishing fleet. Ships from all over Europe had converged on St. Paul Island to partake in spring fishing. They came from France, Spain, Norway and Portugal, with factory ships for onboard fish-processing. There were so many ships that it was difficult to count them. They even came prepared to deal with any possible sickness or injury among the fisherman: a hospital ship was part of the fleet. A large and beautiful ship to behold, this vessel was spectacular when it was lit up at night.

Since there were no restrictions on foreign fishing in Canadian waters at that time, these ships came as close to the island as they wished. At times they fished so near the light station that we could hear the voices of crew on deck as they worked their nets. I would often watch all this activity and wonder how there could be enough fish in the ocean to supply their needs and still be some left for us.

Soon after, in stark contrast, the tiny fishing boats of Neil's Harbour ventured out to the island to catch codfish and halibut. These boats were well-known to us, as were their owners and skippers, men such as Wilson Ingraham, Clifford Smith, and Ron Ingraham. We always looked forward to their arrival, as they brought the mail that had accumulated over the past several months. If the sea remained calm and no strong winds were forecast, they would spend the night anchored in a sheltered corner of Atlantic Cove.

My parents would always do something special when the Neil's Harbour boats were in. Sometimes, if one of these boats was moored in the cove, Mom would cook up a large meal and Dad would invite the crew, usually three or four men, up to the house for dinner. After the meal, the men would sit back and tell us all the news from home. This was a delightful occasion for everyone, especially for my family after the long cold winter and isolation. It was seldom that any visitor came and left without having experienced at least one unusual event. Perhaps it was just the nature of the island, but something always seemed to happen whenever we extended a hand of friendship.

One evening we noticed the *Judy Garland* anchored in Atlantic Cove. Dad rowed out to the fishing boat and invited the captain, Wilson Ingraham, and his three crewmen up to the house for supper. After they accepted our invitation, we hitched up the wagon as the box seat on the back of the tractor would not hold four men.

We had barely passed the halfway point on the trail when an accident occurred, as it did with that first load of coal. Upon hearing that familiar thump, we turned around to see a wagonload of men rolling backwards down the hill. In an instant all the men jumped from the runaway wagon. Wilson picked up the long hitch of the wagon in order to steer it safely down the hill but he had to run faster and faster just to keep up. The other men did their best to slow the descent, until the wagon finally came to a rest at the bottom of the grade. Men less agile would have ridden the wagon to their death, or at least the wagon would have been lost over the cliff. Years of working aboard small boats in changeable waters had made this crew fit and ready for anything. They enjoyed the supper Mom prepared, and would never forget the St. Paul Island roller coaster ride.

The sea was in our blood, and though we were surrounded by ocean the only thing we had done so far was watch other people fish. My father felt that it was about time for us to do a little fishing. However, we needed a boat and fishing gear. There was a damaged Cape Cod dory at the landing that we could use, if we could find some way to repair it. It was about eighteen feet long and featured a stern nearly as sharp as its bow. It had been used by the radio operators, but the last time they used the boom and winch to hoist it out of the water, the stern of the boat struck the cliff. The blow caused a portion of the bottom to separate from the sides. The rest of the boat was still in relatively good shape.

With a little modification, it could be made seaworthy again. Using only a handsaw, Dad sawed off the damaged stern section, leaving the hull about four feet shorter. Then he fashioned a more traditional stern out of some pine stock and nailed it into place. After he caulked the seams and painted the boat, we were ready for a trial run.

Dad purchased an outboard engine, which he, moments after it arrived by fishing boat, eagerly fastened securely to the stern of our boat. This was the first time I

Our modified Cape Cod dory.

had ever seen such a motor, and I was apprehensive. To make matters worse, Dad showed me a picture of one being used on a boat in a comic strip. Depicted in exaggerated form with "Dagwood" operating the motor, the boat was speeding along while nearly standing on end. Remembering that picture, I refused to take the maiden voyage. But I was soon impressed by the way this modified dory performed. The boat moved at a comfortable pace, appeared stable, and, most importantly, didn't stand on end. Convinced that it was safe, I got on board with Dad and we motored around the cove.

Early one morning we noticed schools of herring surfacing all over the cove. The fish had come looking for us before we were finished preparing. Not wanting to miss the opportunity, Dad picked up an old herring net (left to him by my great-grandfather) and tossed it into the boat. With me seated in the stern, my father rowed out to a tiny island a few yards offshore and secured one end of the net to a rock. He ordered me to row straight across the cove while he strung out the net behind the boat. That was a tall order for someone only eight years old who did not know how to row. I took hold of the oars and did my best. The oars did not stroke with a rhythmic beat, nor did the boat slice through the water with ease, but somehow we went the distance and the net was set. This accomplishment gave me little pride: I was uncertain whether I had actually rowed the boat or if it just more or less drifted across the cove.

Then my father tossed a fist-sized rock into the water. The noise startled the fish, causing them to dart toward the open ocean and right into the net. In an instant hundreds of herring were caught in the mesh. We hauled in the net and rowed ashore. In the bottom of the boat scores of silvery blue fish were still flipping around. We cleaned and salted the entire catch. Later some of it would be eaten but most would be used as lobster bait.

It was early June, and I was looking forward to catching lobsters and codfish. However, this conflicted with our time to get away for a few weeks. It was during this time of the year that my father took his annual vacation. Before we were able to leave, however, there would have to be a replacement lightkeeper in my dad's place. It was left to my father to find someone.

Dad, Shepard Malony, Ina and me, with King and Prince. (Photo by Edith Budge)

I felt my father had chosen the right man for the job the first time I met Shepard Malony. He seemed to be in love with the island from the moment he stepped ashore. Although about sixty years old, he looked much younger. His tall, slender body climbed over the rocks with ease; there was little grey in his curly black hair. He had a lively sense of humour and a quick wit, and knew a story for every occasion. He stayed with us several nights before we left. I marvelled that he never ran out of funny stories. Even King liked him; this was most important as the dog would stay on the island while we were on holiday. When our boat pulled away from the cove, the two of them were watching from the edge of the cliff. Shepard was still laughing.

I was excited to be going ashore. I looked forward to seeing my friends and relatives again. Grandfather was waiting to meet us on the wharf, standing there in the same place where I had last seen him. It was an exciting time, for I had much to tell about life on St. Paul Island. The time spent with my grandparents was most enjoyable, but Neil's Harbour wasn't really home anymore. Our vacation passed quickly, but still I was anxious to return to the island, where in my young mind, it was all happening.

When we entered Atlantic Cove on our return, we found that things were indeed beginning to happen. Men and machinery were converging on the wireless station, and things on St. Paul would never be the same again.

7

End of an Era

One of the changes that had taken place in our absence was apparent the moment we stepped ashore that calm July morning in 1956. The Cairns family had departed for the mainland and would not be return-ing. Stan Cairns was replaced by another man, Wilbur Smith, who stayed just long enough to see the wireless station dismantled and closed permanently. The federal government had decided that modern navigational equipment made VGS (the station call letters) unneces-sary. After 122 years of operation, the wireless station at Atlantic Cove would fall silent. There would be no ceremony to mark its closing, nor any awards presented to honour the brave men who had served so well in the time when the station was essential.

Tucked into the curve of low hills, the meadow above Atlantic Cove was the only sheltered site on the entire island. This, no doubt, influ-enced the Nova Scotia lifesaving crew's choice of this site for their head-quarters. The cliffs surrounding it range from twenty to thirty feet high, some of the lowest on the island. There were also a couple of gravel beaches from which a lifeboat could be launched for rescue operations. The terrain around Atlantic Cove was suitable for the construction of houses, and there was enough soil for a vegetable garden.

Atlantic Cove as it appeared around 1908. (H.W. Jones photo).

In the summer, one could be lulled into thinking that this was Paradise. But the first men who came to set up lifesaving operations here in 1832 found it quite the contrary. The hostile environment, the isolation – the loneliness alone was enough to discourage many from serving with the lifesaving force. Their assignment was difficult, dangerous, and often futile. Furthermore, they would have to cope with the psychological impact of dealing with major loss of life under tragic circumstances.

Unlike our family, which came to St. Paul to *prevent* shipwrecks, these men came to deal with the aftermath of the inevitable. In order to facilitate operations, they cut walking trails around the island. These were used daily by coastal patrols in search of shipwrecks. The men from the New Brunswick lifesaving station cut out similar trails on the opposite side of the island; these trails eventually joined those from Atlantic Cove. In this way, the two teams covered the entire island.

In spite of the island's tragic reputation, it was not always a drama of doom and gloom that was played out here at Atlantic Cove. There were many fortunate sailors who owed their lives to the men of this station. In 1863 the Allen steamer *Norwegian* ran aground about a mile north of the Nova Scotia base. A well-organized rescue operation under the command of Governor Samuel Campbell saved the lives of all 550 souls on board.

There is little or no evidence on the ground to indicate that anything of tragic proportions ever occurred here, even though most of the significant wrecks took place within a mile of the rescue station. Above the cliffs of Atlantic Cove, and at the foot of the hill on which the dwelling houses are located, lies a small field. It is a flat grassy meadow, the only substantial area of level ground on the entire island. At the northern end of the field stands a lone headstone. It marks the graves of two small children, Eric and Violet, twin babies of George P. Laing, a radio operator who served at the station in 1938. It is believed the children were already ill when they moved to the island because both died a short time after, at the age of five months. Even though they were dead and perhaps forgotten, I felt a sense of sadness. They would be truly alone here after the station closed.

This solitary monument is something of an illusion. It marks the place where two infants sleep beneath the sod, but they do not sleep alone. In the same field, just a few paces to the west of their headstone, are buried the remains of more than four hundred Irish immigrants who drowned when their ship, the *Pallas*, ran aground near this site in 1856. As the victims washed ashore they were buried together in trenches, in order to dispose of the bodies as quickly as possible. Before the tragedy they were dreaming of a life in the new world, yet found only death on this desolate island.

Around the point and just beyond the monument, there is another mass burial plot. Now unmarked, it was once enclosed by a picket fence. It contains the remains of most of the passengers and crew of the *Royal Sovereign*. Victims of countless other shipwrecks also found their final resting place in this lonely and neglected cemetery. If all those who were laid to rest in this small field had their own headstone, one could scarcely walk between them. They lie here without as much as a single solitary cross or monument to mark their final resting place, a people forgotten by the world and remembered only by God.

The life saving crew preparing to launch their dory. Samuel Cunard Campbell, govenor of the island, is at the steering oar. (Photo by H.W. Jones circa 1908)

Members of the life saving crew about 1908. (Photo by H.W. Jones)

The days of shipwrecks and tragedies were already over when we arrived. The lifesaving crews had come and gone, replaced by the radio operators. Now the wireless station would also close.

For now, the sound of much activity was coming from the structures above the cove. A crew from Halifax was dismantling the station piece by piece. All of the engines and generators were being unbolted from their bases and packed in large wooden crates for shipment to the mainland. Each crate was stencilled with the letters "O.I.C." meaning Officer-in-Charge. My father spent considerable time hauling these boxes down the hill with the tractor. They were unloaded at the winch building, from which they would later be lowered into a landing craft.

In the days that followed there was much activity at the site, but for Ina and me the most exciting event was yet to happen. The mast for all the radio antennas was to be removed. This eighty-foot high steel skeleton tower was supported by a series of anchor cables. Since the riggers were without the service of a crane to lower the mast, a decision was made to simply let it fall to the ground. The workers spent several days preparing the site: trees were cut and the resulting brush placed on the ground where the mast was expected to fall. The intent was to salvage the mast; they hoped the brush would prevent damage by absorbing the impact when the tower hit the ground.

Finally, the day came for the felling of the mast. Our family came down to the station to watch it come crashing to the ground. Ina and I even brought along notepads and pencils in order to sketch the event on paper. Robert Lake, the man in charge of dismantling the station, also supervised the felling of the tower. He had several of his men disconnect only the key anchor wires, enabling the mast to fall in the chosen direction. It began to lean slightly. The men held the cables and, using hand signals, Mr. Lake directed them as they steered the declining tower in the chosen direction.

Finally, when the men could barely hold the mast, Mr. Lake gave the command to release the lines. The tower struck the ground with a bang. The concussion sent a cloud of brush and debris into the air. We all rushed over to find that it had fallen exactly on the mark and sustained very little damage. Robert Lake had proven, even though he had little equipment with which to work, he could do a safe and effective job.

Two items were being left behind for our use on the Southwest. Because there would be little use for a kerosene refrigerator anywhere else, they decided to leave it with us. For Ina and me this meant that we could freeze water and make our own ice cream in the summer. Previously we had to wait until winter to enjoy such a treat. My parents would no longer have to be concerned about keeping meat products fresh when the weather turned mild. One of Lake's men called the old refrigerator obsolete junk, a classic example of that old adage, "One man's trash is another man's treasure."

With a little help, we loaded the fridge on the wagon and headed home with our prize. We put it in the long mud room outside the kitchen door because there was little room in the kitchen for such a machine. Perhaps my father felt it was a little too dangerous to have it in the living quarters of the house: the fridge had to be lit. In order to do that, Dad opened a door at the base of the machine and pulled out the fuel tank that was hinged on one corner. After he filled this flat container with kerosene, he continued to pull it out until a lamp assembly appeared at the far corner. With its round wick it resembled a household kerosene lantern without the tall glass shade. After the wick was lit, the tank was pushed back into the unit and the door was closed. I was always puzzled as to how a fire burning at the base of the machine could keep things cold, even frozen. In fact, it was adjusted in such a way that it behaved like a freezer: it froze everything inside from top to bottom.

The second item left with us was an old generator, allowing us to produce our own electricity. There was no point in ordering a shipment of electrical appliances, though. It was a direct current generator, and most electrical devices operate on alternating current. It was not entirely useless power, however, as it did allow us from time to time to have electric lights inside the house. This generator was not designed to be run continuously, and there were many times when it would not run at all. We started the motor with a hand crank, and all too often our arms ran out of power before the generator started producing any. When it was operating properly we could enjoy the novelty of bright light from two bare bulbs dangling from a wire stretched across the living room ceiling.

On the morning of August 23, 1956, we awoke to find the *Lady Laurier* anchored off the landing. This was the last day for the wireless station at Atlantic Cove. The many containers of equipment, stamped, sealed and tagged, were piled at the edge of the cliff when we arrived at the landing for the final farewell.

While the men were busy loading the barge, my parents said goodbye to the operators. Earl O'Halloran was leaving for Canso, Nova Scotia, to resume his position as radio operator at that site. He must have sensed my interest in his wood carvings: he left me the pattern for the Buckingham Palace guard.

Wilbur Smith, the man who replaced Stan Cairns just a few months before, was here with his wife Avis and their ten-month-old baby, Avis May. They were going to Yarmouth, Nova Scotia, where Wilbur would continue to serve as a radio operator for many more years.

Avis and my mother had become good friends during their short stay, and I could see that Mom was having trouble saying goodbye.

With the last radio operators finally on board, the barge departed for the ship. From the barge's wake two waves rolled across the cove like a curtain being slowly drawn across a stage after a great performance. On the hillside above the bay, two houses stood empty and alone, seeming to stare down in disbelief.

With the exception of the lightkeepers on the Northeast, that little rock at the other end of the island, we were alone on St. Paul. The island proper was now all ours to guard and to keep. At the end of the day, Dad summed up this event in the station log book with these simple words: "August 23, 1956. VGS closed today."

8

Living on the Edge

A year had passed since we first set foot on St. Paul Island. It was mid-September. Four seasons had dealt their hands of fury, peace, cold, and warmth, and we had survived them all. The obsolete and out-dated equipment that was vital to our needs had been improved upon, as far as circumstance would allow. Life on the rock had become routine, but never ordinary. We learned to expect the unexpected, and if anything seemed reasonable, it was probably not. My mother's failure to think in this manner nearly led to my death.

Just before daybreak on September 15, 1956, the supply ship *Lady Laurier* arrived at the island with the annual shipment of groceries and supplies for the light station. While I slept, my father watched the lights of the approaching ship from the kitchen window. By the time I awoke, Dad had already left for the landing on the tractor. He wanted to be there early to start up the winch engine, ready for the first boatload of supplies to be hoisted ashore.

This was an exciting time for me, and I was upset when I discovered that my father had gone without me.

"There's no time to eat breakfast this morning," I said, pulling on my mother's arm and pushing Ina toward the door. "We gotta start walking now!"

We hiked down the trail through the dull and overcast morning, me doing my best to hurry Mom and Ina along. I desperately wanted to leave them behind and run ahead. I looked back impatiently and saw my mother. She was holding Ina's hand, limping along as fast as she could, her body swaying from side to side with her uneven gait.

There was really no need to hurry. I could tell by the sound of the winch that the landing operation had not yet begun. The winch was driven by an engine similar to the one-lungers in the fishing boats back in Neil's Harbour. Its one large cylinder emitted that same loud popping sound from the exhaust. If the engine was idling and no load was applied to the winch, it produced a steady rhythmic beat. If supplies were being hoisted, the strain on the winch caused the engine to produce louder, further spaced, somewhat irregular snaps. The steady, even beat from the engine told me I wasn't missing anything.

We arrived just as the landing operation began and I was content to watch the activity from a safe distance at the cliff's edge. I stood where I could see both the men in the barge below the cliff and those at the top operating the winch and boom.

The first load to come up was our yearly supply of groceries. The boxes were placed carefully in slings before being hoisted. The food supplies appeared to be rather light as the engine did not seem to labour much under the weight. Seeing little danger in this operation and not content with watching from a distance, I tugged my mother's sleeve and said, "Can I move in a little closer for a better look?"

"No, Billy," she said. "It's too dangerous to stand near that boom in case it breaks." Then she reminded me about the heavier items yet to come up. I accepted that she had reason to be concerned and returned to my previous position.

I watched the men as they placed bags of heavy coal into the slings and listened to the sound of the engine as it laboured under the strain of the lift. After the coal, the crew turned their attention to the drums of fuel oil. At first they were lifting them two at once, but must have felt it was unsafe and began to hoist them one barrel at a time. Finally, with everything ashore that was going ashore, the only task remaining was to return last year's empties. Empty fuel barrels from the last year had to be returned to Halifax for refilling.

Loading the barrels was fast and simple. The empty drums were rolled into position, lifted off the grass with the boom, and then swung out over the cliff. The winch operator then released the brake, lowering the barrels into the barge below.

The loading operation. (Sketch by Vernon Amos)

Convinced that it was now finally safe to move in closer, I ran over to my mother again. "Is it safe to stand beside the building now and watch? All the heavy stuff is ashore."

She thought carefully for a moment, then said, "If the boom didn't break under the strain of all those heavy loads, I can't see any problem with lowering empty barrels."

As I ran off she cautioned me again, saying, "Stay out of the way, and be careful."

I quickly sought the best vantage point, directly under the boom when it was in the swung-out position. Standing near the edge of the cliff, I could see the whole operation while not interfering with any of the workers. About thirty feet to my right a man was standing at the end of the building, holding a rope in his hand. The rope was attached to the far end of the boom. His job was to pull the boom out over the cliff at the appropriate time and release the necessary slack, when a second man on the opposite side pulled it in over the grass. That second man was positioned about forty-five feet to my left. The only other crewman to be concerned about was the winch operator, and I was careful not to obstruct his view.

The final operation was going well and the last few drums were rolled into position. Then one of the crew changed the routine. Perhaps to save time, he pulled in the boom before the winch operator had time

Two views of the "landing" with the remains of the boom building and winch at the edge of the cliff. (Photos by Billy Budge)

to raise the empty hook all the way to the top. The hook slid and bounced along the wall of the cliff during the last few feet of its ascent.

A few more loads were taken up without incident. Suddenly, the hook slipped into a crevice in the cliff and became wedged there. The power of the winch on the cable caused the boom to be swept violently back out over the trapped hook, ripping the rope from the hand of the man who had been holding it in. The boom stopped directly over my head.

I looked up and saw the large wooden beam beginning to whip under the increasing strain. The cable beneath it was vibrating so intensely that it slapped against the boom with a deafening sound.

Instinct told me to run, but my feet seemed to be caught in something. I was too busy observing the scene above my head to study the situation at my feet. Anyway, help was on the way – I saw the man on my left coming toward me with outstretched arms. When he was almost close enough to grab me, he looked up and saw something that made him turn back. The man on the right tried to rescue me as well, but when he looked up, he too made a hasty retreat. Even though the boom was a very smooth and carefully finished beam, pieces were now beginning to fracture, and large fragments were falling on me. The spectre of the splintering boom unnerved the crewmen and they decided to leave me to the hands of fate.

Meanwhile, inside the building, the operator of the winch was in a state of panic and confusion, unable to understand how an empty hook could possibly be ripping everything apart. The operator could have easily corrected the situation using only one hand or one foot. By releasing the clutch lever that he was holding in his hand, he would have disconnected the winch from the engine, thus releasing the strain on the cable; with his foot, he could have jumped on the brake and halted everything. But he did neither, and the winch continued to reel in the cable.

Outside, I was still struggling to escape, but couldn't free my feet from the mysterious trap. Extremely loud popping from the exhaust of the engine indicated that something was about to give. With a loud crash, the boom finally broke. I had just enough time to realize my life was over before blacking out.

The first thing I saw, when I regained consciousness a few moments later, was my father and all the crew looking down at me. Someone was wiping a bloody handkerchief across my face. The only injury I had sustained was a bruised nose, which was bleeding mightily.

I had been struck by a small section of the broken boom, with only enough force to knock me out. When the boom broke, there was no longer any pressure on the bottom section. It simply fell on me with only the force of its own weight. The top half, however, came crashing down with tremendous force, and would have struck me had I moved from my position. I owed my life to a short piece of forgotten cable, which had snared my foot and prevented me from making that fatal step.

A few feet away, my mother was lying on the grass where, believing I was dead, she had fallen in a dead faint. As *Lady Laurier's* crew left that evening, each man in turn reminded me of how lucky I was to be alive. If St. Paul Island were looking to claim another victim, it would have to wait.

My mother had her brush with fate during the winter of 1958. Dad and I were just returning to the station from a Monday morning duck hunting trip. We both heard it at the same time, more clearly when there was a lull in the wind. The sound was coming from our house. We were still some distance away when we realized it was my mother's voice. It was almost noon, but this did not sound like a call for lunch: it was a frantic cry for help! We heard it again, more clearly now – "Freddy, help, Freddy!" I had never seen my father run as fast as he did those last few hundred yards.

Something must be terribly wrong. I thought first of Ina – perhaps she was playing too close to the edge of the cliff and had fallen over. Recently, Ina had shocked the family by coming into the house carrying my .22 calibre rifle with several bullets in her pocket. She said she had gone out hunting alone but did not see any ducks. This incident caught my parents off guard – Ina had no previous interest in ducks, guns, or hunting. But after the scolding she received for this unusual behaviour, it was doubtful that she would try it again.

Dad was thinking that it was my mother who was in trouble. It was Monday, the day she always did the laundry with her trusty gasoline washing machine. Perhaps she had accidentally caught her hand in the wringer which had happened before, when we lived in Neil's Harbour.

My mother had been busy with her washing when we left earlier that morning to duck hunt. Dad had started the washer before we left, because Mom was unable to start it herself. Unlike modern small gas engines, the washing machine did not have a retractable start cord. The pull cord hung on a nail driven in the wall beside the washing machine. You had to wrap the cord around the start pulley several times and then, with a quick pull on the handle, the machine would usually start. Mom could never seem to pull it with enough force to start it. It was unlikely she had injured herself doing this because she wouldn't even attempt it.

Only a few strides from the house, we witnessed a terrifying scene. My mother ran across the deck, screaming, apparently on fire. Then we saw the gas can in her hand, and realized it was the can of gas that was burning. She dropped the burning can on the step and grabbed a shovel lying nearby. She began pounding on the can with the shovel in hopes of extinguishing the fire. I had watched my grandfather control a grass fire near his home in this manner, but it was evident that a shovel was not going to extinguish a gas fire.

Mom was creating a fine display of fireworks with her shovel. Each time she struck the can, burning gas flew into the air and splashed over the deck, where it continued to burn. Even the rocks beside the doorstep appeared to be burning. In her state of panic, she had given no thought to the possibility of her clothes igniting from the flaming splashes.

My father reached her and quickly took control of the scene. He picked up a heavy doormat lying on the step and tossed it over the burning can. Deprived of oxygen, the fire went out instantly. After nature cooled down the can (and Dad cooled down my mother), it was time to investigate the cause of the fire.

Determining the cause of the fire was the easy part; deciding who was to blame was never resolved. When my father started the washing machine, he failed to check the quantity of gas in the tank. Before my mother finished her laundry, she realized the motor was running out of fuel. Since she knew it was impossible for her to restart the motor after it had stopped, she decided to refuel it while it was still running. Before the job was finished, a spark from the exhaust ignited the can of gas. She dropped the burning can and ran outside, calling for help. Suddenly she realized if she left the burning can on the floor, the house would catch fire. One of my mother's greatest fears was that the house would burn down during the winter, leaving us with no food, clothing, or shelter except for those abandoned dwellings at the landing. She went back into the house, picked up the flaming gas can, and ran outside.

In the end, it didn't matter who was to blame, for Mom had truly saved our house from being destroyed by fire.

Later that same winter, my mother went another round with the washer, and this time it was a knockout. Everyone was at home and I was busy with schoolwork. In the back room across the hall, Mom was doing the laundry. I thought that the machine was making more noise than usual, but made no comment to anyone about it. A short time later, Mom came into the kitchen to pick up another basket of clothes. The noise must have been disturbing to my father as well, for he asked, "How much more laundry do you have left to do, Edith?"

She replied, "I have only ...." and collapsed unconscious to the floor!

Dad picked her up in his arms and ran outside. In the fresh air, she quickly regained consciousness. We went inside to investigate the cause of her collapse. This time my mother's misfortune was due to no fault of her own. However, the incident might have been prevented had someone taken the time to check a small fitting on the motor. This fitting held the exhaust pipe on the machine and was of vital importance to safety. The vibrating of the washing machine had caused the exhaust pipe, normally vented outside, to separate from the engine. Toxic fumes slowly leaked from the separation and filled the room. My mother had collapsed from carbon monoxide poisoning. If Dad and I had gone off hunting that morning, we might well have returned home to find both my mother and Ina dead inside the house.

By nature St. Paul Island is a dangerous place and pets too must tread cautiously. My mother, feeling bad for Ina, who had no human playmates, determined that her daughter should have a pet. It came out by fishing boat in the spring of 1957, just a small grey ball of fur of no particular breed, a kitten that Ina loved and cared for like a mother raising a child. She named it Fluffy, and they quickly became inseparable. No matter where we were or what we did, if Ina was there, so was Fluffy.

On a crisp fall morning the following year, Dad and I were in the workshop preparing for winter. Several barrels of kerosene were used throughout the season to fuel the living room stove, the lamps, the refrigerator, and of course, the light. We could have used the kerosene one barrel at a time, as we did gas for the tractor, but this was inconvenient for household fuel. The barrel would always seem to run empty at the most inopportune time, like on frosty, stormy days.

The barrels were stored outdoors, and each new one had to be prepared for use separately. First, the faucet had to be removed from the empty drum and placed on a full one. Then, using two planks for a ramp, the fresh barrel would be rolled on to the stand. After it was positioned faucet-side down, it was ready for use. It was not an easy task, especially if the full drum was frozen in the ice.

To keep refills to a minimum, one large tank had been installed inside the workshop. More than three feet in diameter, it was mounted vertically against the wall at the end of the workbench. It had a four barrel capacity, and when filled provided the station with enough fuel for the entire winter. You had only to place a container at the base of the tank, turn the valve, and drain off what you needed.

On this particular morning, we were inside the workshop filling the tank for the winter. Dad stood on a stool and began by removing the cover (similar to that used on a garbage can). A hand pump was installed on the barrel and using a hose, we pumped the kerosene from the barrel into the large tank.

We had emptied several barrels and the tank was nearly full when Ina came into the workshop.

"I want to have a turn working the pump, too," she said.

Dad agreed, and maybe it was because we were both watching how awkwardly she turned the crank on the pump that we did not see Fluffy enter the building. Neither did we see her leap up on the bench and crouch down in preparation for the final pounce to the top of the (uncovered!) tank. The fuel tank sat next to a window, and on sunny days the top of it would be bathed in sunlight. The cat liked to lie on top of the tank and sleep in the warmth.

We all heard the splash, and we all knew what had happened. Dad jumped up on the stool, expecting to see the cat swimming in the kerosene. To his surprise, he found the cat was not swimming – she was circulating around at the bottom of the tank. She looked something like a dolphin at Disney World, but I suspect not having as much fun. Dad tried to grab the cat as she darted around, but she never came close enough to the surface to be within reach. With time running out, and no dip net available, it looked as though Fluffy would surely drown.

Dad pulled out all the stops when he saw Ina crying on the floor. Tears were streaming down her face and she kept repeating the same words, "She gonna be dead!"

Seeing her grief, Dad plunged his face into the kerosene in order to extend his reach. Seconds later he stood up shaking his head and spitting kerosene. In his outstretched hand he grasped the drenched and limp cat. Barely alive, "Fluffy" was anything but.

Mom came out and took the cat into the house to begin "Operation Scrubdown." Yet no matter how many times Mom bathed the cat in warm, soapy water, Fluffy still came out smelling like kerosene. Furthermore, the cat became very ill. There were several times during the next few days when she was very near death. She kept vomiting kerosene and was constantly coughing.

As the weeks went by, Fluffy slowly recovered from her oily ordeal. However, she never completely regained her health: she even seemed to have developed some deformities. Her body had more curves than it did prior to its immersion. In spite of this, she didn't seem to be having any pain and continued to enjoy life, doing what cats do. In the future, we would always remember to make sure Fluffy was not around when the fuel tank was uncovered. A valuable lesson was learned by all: cats apparently do not swim well in kerosene.

On those winter days between school hours and hunting, Ina and I would often entertain ourselves outdoors. We would build snow forts and igloos, and make snow-sculpture horses. We built our igloos similar to those pictured in one of our school textbooks, with a dome shape. Unlike the Eskimos, who used hard-packed dry snow, we preferred to use wet, sticky snow for ease of construction and especially for closing in the roof. Our snow horses were built with four individual legs and we could climb up and sit on their backs and pretend to ride off into the sunset like Roy Rogers. When the weather turned colder these projects froze solid and often lasted all winter.

Nothing was more fun than sliding, but it was also extremely dangerous. However, if we were exceedingly careful, we could indulge in a limited amount of this exciting sport. We would always have to be aware of the unforgiving cliff at the base of the slope just below our house.

One bright morning in early spring, when the hard crust of late winter snow still covered the ground, Ina and I decided to take advantage of this fast surface. We plotted a safe course to follow, and at the end of the run we planned to strike the fence at a wide angle, thus avoiding any sudden stop that could result in an injury to ourselves or damage to the sleigh. Since Dad and I had long since replaced the old rotten fence that had greeted us when we first arrived, it would seem that we had an effective backstop situated a safe distance from the cliff.

We retrieved from the loft of the tractor garage that same sleigh that Dad had built the first winter we spent on the island. It was still in perfect shape, having been used only once or twice by King, hauling supplies (and chasing rabbits). It was quite heavy, but together Ina and I could pull it easily across the hard snow.

We towed the sleigh up the hill as far as the treeline behind the house, and got ready for the first run. We flew down the hill like lightning and ricocheted off the fence, just as we had planned. After several runs I began to feel quite confident. Our parents also seemed comfortable with our activity. I saw them from time to time watching through the kitchen window and they didn't seem to be concerned.

It was later that same afternoon when the inevitable happened. We had failed to notice that nails in the fence poles were slowly coming out, as a result of the steady bombardment from the sleigh. On that last trip down the hill, our sled went straight through the fence, blasting two poles ahead of us. It took me a second or two to realize just what had happened, and where we were headed. I pushed Ina off the sleigh to the right and I rolled off to the left only a few feet from the edge. There was only silence as the sled sailed through the air and over the cliff. We couldn't, from our viewpoint, see it crash into the ocean below – we only heard the hollow echo of its splash.

Ina and I were shakily relieved to have escaped the sleigh-ride of death. I was sure that when we relayed the news to our parents, they would be happier with our survival than angry about our dangerous activity. We ran up to the house to tell them about our close call.

Dad, when he was satisfied that we were okay, rushed out the door with his duck-retriever device in his hand, hoping to recover the sleigh. The sleigh was drifting with the tide and would soon pass a small point just beyond the cliff. My father hoped to retrieve it from here as it floated past. When he got out on the point, the sleigh was beyond his tossing range. There was nothing he could do except watch it drift out to sea until it disappeared. Later that evening, I noticed that Mom was visibly shaken by the near tragedy and Dad was still upset over the loss of his sleigh.

Little did I know, I would have another encounter with this same cliff. This time, I would go over.

It was a cold and wintry morning with a strong northwest wind. I was groping my way along the fence that ran between our house and the lighthouse. I was wearing my only cap, the ear-lugs pulled down to protect me from the bitter cold. Suddenly, I lost my balance and was slammed against the fence by a strong gust. The impact jolted the cap from my head, then the wind sent it flying high into the air. When it came down, it disappeared over the same cliff that only a year before had swallowed our sleigh.

With no spare headgear available, my mother was forced to improvise. As a temporary substitute for a cap, she wrapped a cloth around my head and somehow secured the ends. It looked like a turban. Even though it provided the necessary protection, I was most unhappy with it. I could not put it on myself, and if it came unwrapped I would have to hold it together until I got home. I decided that something else had to be done.

On a bright, calm Sunday morning a few days later, I hiked down to the point beyond our house and climbed down onto the rocks. From there I peered into the cove beneath the cliff and saw a miracle. Sitting on a ledge of rock at the base of the cliff, just a few feet above sea level, was my trusty blue cap. I had only to retrieve it.

I rushed home and broke the good news to my father, then convinced him to get a long piece of rope. He tied it around the upper portion of my body, and we positioned ourselves at the edge of the cliff directly above the cap. The steep slope above the cliff made it dangerous to even walk near the edge. It would be impossible for my father to lower me down on a rope and still maintain his balance. Dad solved this problem by using another piece of rope to secure himself to one of the fence posts about thirty feet up the slope. Once Dad was confident of his stability while holding the rope, I backed out over the edge and he slowly lowered me down. Once I reached the cap, I placed it on my head and signalled for him to pull me up. If I never made it safely to the top, at least I would go out with my cap on.

In a few places on the way up, I was able to assist by gaining a foothold, but for the most part, it was a complete lift for my father. Finally, I scrambled over the top, unscathed, and with my cap still on my head. I had challenged that formidable cliff and won.

9

Summer on St. Paul

There was a sense of freedom that came after the last sheet of drift ice had slipped away from the island. Warm spring breezes would have melted the snow that had held our tractor captive in the garage for the past several months. Our roaming was no longer restricted to the immediate vicinity of the light station. We could now explore the entire island on foot, or by water if the weather was favourable.

More important than simply getting out or walking around was the need to talk to someone different. Aside from a brief word with crewmen from a passing supply ship as they tossed us a parcel, we had not come face-to-face with another human since November of the previous year. On the Northeast, only three miles away, there were people who could also use some company. It was one of our first spring priorities to pay them a visit. On the first day that the sea was calm enough, we planned to launch our boat from the slip at Atlantic Cove and motor north along the coast to the other light station.

One year, a near perfect morning in early May inspired Dad to seize the opportunity and make that first visit to the Northeast. Winds were light when we all piled onto the tractor and motored down the trail toward the landing. Only small patches of snow remained on the road, and the ocean had been free of heavy drift ice for more than a week. We were most anxious to launch the boat, fire up the motor, and enjoy the freedom of the sea.

That trip was probably the only time that I was more interested in the actual visit with the lightkeeper than in the voyage up the coast. We had heard that he was enjoying something on that little rock that we could only dream about at the Southwest. Since they had the advantage of electricity produced by A.C. generators operating twenty-four hours a day, they could also enjoy the latest fad: television. Joe Mitchell, the lightkeeper in charge, had acquired a set for himself. We understood that his family had watched it all winter, even though Joe described the signal as being "a little weak." Television on St. Paul Island seemed too good to be true, but with a little luck we could find ourselves sitting in front of a TV watching a movie that same afternoon.

Only a few homes in Neil's Harbour had a television when we lived there, and we were not one of them. From time to time, I did gather with other kids to watch TV at someone else's home. Though I hadn't missed that form of entertainment when we moved to the island, it would be a welcome treat to see it again.

At the landing, we saw that nature was not cooperating with our plan. Across the little cove beneath the cliff there was a wall of ice that had formed during the winter and had not yet melted. During the drift-ice season, the waves tossed fragmented particles of ice up on the shore, where they froze into a solid mass. This formed a continuous ridge along the beach and covered the bottom section of the boat ramp. We called this formation a "sea-wall," a familiar sight around the island in the winter but uncommon this late in the spring. It formed in a manner that created a gentle slope up the inside of the wall and a vertical drop on the ocean side. It was not possible to safely launch our boat into the water or haul it up again over this solid ten-foot-high wall. That is, not until we chopped. For several days, Dad and I shared an axe as we hacked at this mountain of ice. Eventually, we succeeded in cutting an opening large enough to safely slide the boat through. Without Dad's determination our trip to the Northeast would not have been possible until a later date.

The modified Cape Cod dory we had used during our first year on St. Paul had been replaced by a slightly larger and heavier craft. It was too heavy to be launched or hoisted out of the water with the boom assembly, leaving us with the boat ramp as our only way out. Little effort was required to launch it down the ramp's steep slope to the water, and quite often we controlled its descent with a piece of rope attached to the bow. The other end was passed once around one of the lateral poles in the ramp, and as the rope was slowly released, the resulting friction against the wooden pole provided the necessary braking action for the boat as it slid down the ways.

Almost a week had passed since our first attempt, but now we felt there was nothing to stop us. Once the boat was afloat, we climbed aboard and Dad pushed off with an oar. After a couple of pulls on the start-cord the outboard motor roared to life, and we were off for the Northeast. Winter's chill still lingered on the breeze. From time to time, Mom pulled the collar of her coat across her face for warmth.

A few small chunks of nearly invisible drift ice still floated just beneath the water's surface. Sometimes a piece would strike against the hull with the force of a sledge hammer. The waves off Norwegian Head seemed to stir in a frenzy of confusion as the sea responded to the effect of wind and tide travelling in opposite directions. Suddenly, around the next point, the Northeast loomed into view and within minutes we were motoring up the calm waters of the tittle.

Ina and I were the first ashore, leaving Dad and Mom to secure the boat to the ramp. We raced up the boardwalk that led to Joe's house. We slowed our pace near the centre of the small island, where part of the boardwalk was a long, narrow bridge suspended high above a gully. The door of the house was slightly open, but we knocked anyway, and stepped into the kitchen. Joe's wife was preparing food on the counter while their two children played on the floor. Inside the living room, Joe was sitting in his favourite chair, near a window that provided him with a clear view of the lighthouse. The Mitchell family was excited and surprised by our unexpected visit.

They were quick to welcome us into their home. When Mom and Dad arrived, they invited all of us into their living room. The television was turned on, but was obviously not tuned in to the right channel. The screen displayed only "snow," and there was no sound. Politely I asked, "Mr Mitchell, would you please tune in the TV so that we can watch something."

"It is on the proper channel," he said. "We were watching a movie when you came in."

"But, sir," I continued, "there's no sound and no picture."

He apologized for there being no sound but then he pointed toward the TV and said, "See that figure on the screen now – I think it's a woman!"

Dad agreed with him, but I could see only a white sparkling screen that blinked from time to time as though a scene was changing somewhere behind the snow.

Lacking the vivid imagination required to watch Joe's TV, I left the house and walked back toward our boat. Ina must have been equally unimpressed with the television because she followed me to the shore. The boat was secured to the ramp with a bowline while a stern anchor held it out from the shore to prevent it from being damaged against the rocks. Dad had left just enough slack in the stern line for us to pull the bow in and climb aboard.

Once the boat slipped back out from the shore, we occupied ourselves doing what we always enjoyed while our parents visited the Mitchells. It was fun to lean over the gunwale, peer through the pristine water of the tittle, and try to identify the various species of fish on the bottom. Perch, sculpin and crabs were always there in abundance, but if we studied the bottom long enough it was often possible to spot a lobster crawling along. After a while, Ina and I would get out Dad's mackerel lines and see if we could catch one of those elusive fish swimming beneath the boat.

Neither of us could swim, but that did not seem to matter. We wore no life jackets to save us if we fell overboard – the boating world of the 1950s wasn't as safety conscious as that of today. If Mother's instructions were heeded, then survival was always assured. In Neil's Harbour, she would say to us, "Don't play on the highway – you'll be run over." On St. Paul Island, her advice was similar: "Don't fall overboard – you'll drown!" Our fear of drowning was enough to keep us safely positioned inside the boat, as long as it remained upright.

While Ina and I fished in the tittle, we were oblivious to a grim reminder of that tragic December day of 1955, when, perhaps, a life jacket could have saved a life. Poised directly above our heads was a concrete pedestal with a portion of steel cable still attached – the cable that had held the boatswain chair. The cable end, now rusted and frayed, still hung down over the cliff where it had come to rest on that fateful morning. It seemed to serve as a memorial to George Gatza, whom it had failed. The assembly wasn't replaced after the accident.

After several hours of visiting at the Northeast, it was time to return to the landing and home. Although the sky was still clear, the shades of evening had descended along our route on the east side of the island. Near the shore, high cliffs cast dark, ominous shadows over calm water. Several bald eagles soared overhead. We could see more perched in the stunted and twisted trees that grew on the steep slope of Norwegian Head. This area was their nesting ground, and it had been well chosen: it was practically impossible for anybody or anything to climb up there and disturb them.

Back at the landing, it would be my responsibility to haul up the boat. For me it was even easier than launching. At the instant the boat struck the bottom ways of the ramp, I leaped over the bow and picked up the cable I had placed there before we left. I slipped the steel hook on the end of the cable through an eyebolt in the stem of the boat.

While the others were climbing out of the boat, I ran up and prepared the other end of the cable for the haul. This operation had to be carried out quickly. At the top of the ramp, the cable passed through a pulley and made a ninety-degree turn to the left. The upper end was lying in the grass near the edge of the cliff, ready to be attached to the tractor. By the time I reached the tractor, Dad would have the boat properly aligned on the ramp. While still standing in the surf, my father had to position the boat upright on an even keel and keep it that way throughout the tow. Waves threatened to pound the boat broadside into the rocks. My father eyed me impatiently as I worked – too long in the surf and he might lose control of the boat. This would mean almost certain injury to himself and possible loss of the boat.

In an instant, I picked up the loop on the end of the cable, flipped it over a pin on the hitch of the tractor, and positioned myself behind the wheel. Although I was too small to drive while sitting in the seat, I had no trouble operating the tractor standing up. I would straddle the transmission housing, using my right foot for the brakes and my left one for the clutch.

By the time I had the tractor started, Mom was already standing in her assigned position. Since I was unable to see either the boat or the ramp due to the obstruction of the cliff, I relied on Mother's hand signals to relay Dad's instructions to me. Standing out of harm's way beside an old winch we used as an anchor for the pulley, Mom had a clear view of the whole operation. Usually there were only two signals – one to start and one to stop when the boat reached the top. I watched carefully for any signal partway up, which might indicate that Dad had slipped and fallen beneath the boat. My mother must have had great confidence in my driving ability because she never seemed concerned about me operating the tractor so close to the edge of the cliff. When the hauling was completed, Dad secured the boat while I coiled the cable ready for the next excursion, when we would repeat the process all over again.

All of us boarded the tractor and made our way slowly up the trail. King, who had waited for our return, jogged along ahead. There was little discussion; in our own minds we all reflected on the day's events. It was refreshing to see other people, even though Joe's television left something to be desired. I teased Dad about his actually seeing a picture on the screen, suggesting that with his imagination he could tune in to his favourite show and watch *Our Miss Brooks* on the radio. Throughout the summer months we would return to the Northeast from time to time, but like ants, it was more important for us to use this season to prepare for winter.

Each year in mid-May the lobster fishery would begin on the mainland. A few boats would venture out to St. Paul to set traps around the island. My father, having been a lobster fisherman himself, used his skill to construct about a dozen traps. Over the years the number of traps we fished increased, as we acquired those abandoned by commercial fishermen at the end of each season. There were various reasons why lobster traps would be abandoned in the water around St. Paul. Often, ropes would become entangled in the bottom, making the traps impossible to haul. Storms sometimes washed the traps in too close to the shore, where heavy surf would prevent a large boat from safely retrieving them. With patience and time on our side, we would eventually recover most stray traps.

On a few occasions, I suspected traps were left behind on purpose. I could never believe it was a coincidence that, for no apparent reason, several traps were left in the same small section of coast where we fished. It was obviously a gift left by some compassionate fisherman to a lightkeeper and his family on this lonely rock. We lost traps as well, but through the process of recovering and repairing, we maintained about twenty.

In order to catch lobsters you need bait, and to get it we used the old herring net. We positioned it just off Atlantic Cove for easy access. As was common for most bait nets, it was anchored on one end while the other end was left free to swing in response to the wind and currents. Each morning before pulling the traps we hauled the net and retrieved whatever herring or mackerel were captured during the previous night. It was important that the corks attached to the top of the net be stretched out in a straight line across the surface of the water. This straight line indicated that all was in order and we needed only to haul the net and reset it.

On more than one occasion we approached the net to find all the corks grouped together in a small cluster. This was an indication of big trouble below. When we drew closer, a ghostly white shadow would suddenly appear in the water beneath the tangled corks. This would be the underside of a large shark that had struck the net during the night, and in an effort to escape, succeeded only in tangling itself in the net. Often the shark was still alive.

It was too difficult and dangerous, working within the confines of our small boat, to free the shark from the net. There was only one safe way to unscramble this mess. We untied the net from its mooring, and secured it to the stern of the boat. Then we towed the net, with the shark still entangled, to the shore. There, using the boom and winch, Dad hoisted up the entire mess and dropped it on the grass. After the final flicker of life had vanished from the shark, we untangled it from the net and towed its body back out to sea. We didn't keep the shark for food. As far as we were concerned, the species was not edible. At that time, there was no commercial shark fishery in Canada; the world had not yet developed a taste for this fish. We repaired the damaged net and returned it to the sea to fish again.

Almost without fail, the net supplied enough fish to replenish the bait in each lobster trap daily. On those days when the net was empty, we used herring or mackerel that we had salted earlier. A third option for bait was to use codfish liver that was slightly rotten and placed inside a bottle with holes punched in the lid. Cod liver oil oozed out of the leaky cover and lobsters were lured into the trap by the odour. Not only did this work well, but this simple bottle of bait would last for many days. However, the same smell that caused the lobsters to crawl into the trap almost caused us to crawl overboard while the trap was in the boat.

All the lobsters we caught were used for food (ours was not a commercial fishery). We usually cooked them the same day, in a large pot over an open fire at the landing site. Shelling and cleaning were done in the comfort of our home, avoiding the biting insects. (In the spring and early summer, the island was infested with a species of mosquito much larger than anything encountered on the mainland.) We ate lobsters until our appetites for this delicacy diminished to the point where we became nauseated at the very thought of lobsters.

Later in the year we would be craving these shellfish again, so we always preserved some for winter. We did this through the magic of canning. Dad acquired an old manually-operated canner with a crank and levers designed to seal specially manufactured covers on cans. He packed each can full of lobster meat before he placed them in the machine. A gentle pull on the lever and a few turns of the crank resulted in a sealed can of cooked lobster meat. Then the cans were ready to be boiled again, to seal them. After several hours of boiling, the cans were ready to be labelled and placed on the shelf for later consumption.

Satisfied that an adequate quantity of lobsters had been preserved for the winter, we began to harvest another bounty from the sea. Cod was perhaps the easiest type of fish to catch, mainly because no bait was required. They were caught by handline, using two types of large lures known as jigs. As in most fishing, choosing a jig was a matter of taste:

one jig *looked* like a small fish, and the other *acted* like a fish. Both worked equally well.

We learned that the ocean floor drops steeply away from the island, enabling us to jig for cod quite close to the shore. Just off Atlantic Cove, and a little way beyond the herring net, was our favourite location. Here the depth was about thirty fathoms (180 feet) which is ideal for cod-jigging.

To catch a cod, first you tossed the jig into the water and lowered it to the bottom by uncoiling the handline off a wooden rack called a reel. When the line stopped running out, it meant that the jig had reached the bottom. Next, it was raised a short distance off the bottom by pulling in an equal amount of line. Then the line is given one quick pull and allowed to run back. This process of constantly pulling and releasing is what is known as jigging. When this sawing motion is interrupted by a sudden resistance on the pull back, it means that a fish has been hooked. The final task is simply to pull the fish to the surface and haul it into the boat. The codfish is not a strong fighter, and unless it is a large one it usually comes to the surface without much of a struggle. Once on location it was usually only a few minutes before we pulled the first codfish over the side.

As with all types of fishing, there were those that got away. One calm and sunny afternoon, my father and I were fishing off Petrie's Point, on the western side of the island. Cod were unusually plentiful that day and we often hooked a fish with the first pluck on the line. After about an hour or so, Dad suggested we quit fishing soon.

We would have to dress, clean, and salt the fish before returning home that evening, a task that would take another couple of hours at least. But it's always difficult to quit when the fish are biting, and I begged him to let me catch one more.

A few minutes later, I hooked a big one. First, I thought my jig was caught on the ocean floor. There seemed to be little or no movement, and I could not pull in the line. Then, little by little, it began to come up. The line squeaked as it slipped through my fingers, and jerked with each kick by the heavy fish. Suddenly, the kicking ceased. The fish seemed to have gotten much smaller. Dad was joking about me working so hard to pull up a small fish.

Dejectedly, I continued pulling, and the jig came up to the side of the boat. I bent over the gunwale . . . and looked into the eyes of the biggest codfish I had ever seen. But a head was all there was! I proudly held the head up for Dad to see. A small portion of the intestines still dangled from beneath the gills. It was obvious that a hungry shark had made a snack out of my large fish en route to the surface.

A few minutes later the shark found the source of his free lunch and surfaced near the boat. It swam back and forth, dorsal fin slicing through the water, as it waited for another fish to come up. It swam in ever-tightening circles around the boat until, finally, it was brushing against the hull. The shark swam up one side of the boat and down the other. A sickening thought occurred to me: only a few minutes before, I had been leaning over the gunwale, washing fish blood off my hands and arms.

This shark had no intention of leaving us alone, even after we quit jigging. It began to nip at the tiny white propeller of the outboard motor whenever it passed the stern. I watched nervously as the motor shook with each assault on the propeller. If we lost the motor and had to row, we would find ourselves at the mercy of the shark. Watching his chance, Dad started the motor and steered the boat toward the shore. The shark followed in our wake. From time to time, it moved in close to bite the rotating prop. It was obvious that there was something on board our boat that it wanted. We had no intentions of donating our fish to its cause, unless, of course, it was required as a substitute for ourselves.

Finally, we were close enough to the shore that we could see the bottom, but the shark would not quit the chase. Only when the boat entered very shallow water did he finally give up and head back to the open sea. Sharks, by nature, are unpredictable, and this caused us some concern. Yet this one was never violently aggressive at any time during the pursuit. I think he was just curious, or maybe wanted to clean his teeth on the propeller, as though it were a giant toothbrush for a big fish.

This was not the first, nor the last, encounter we had with sharks. We often hooked them accidentally with the cod jig and pulled them to the surface. Because they always swam up willingly with the jig in their mouth, there was no indication that you had caught anything especially large. I was quite surprised the first time I looked over the side and saw that the fish I had just hauled up was as big as the boat. Each time this happened, I passed my fishing line to Dad, who seemed to have developed a skill for jerking the hook from the mouth of a shark. These were "big ones that got away," and I was glad they did.

Cod fishing was often a family activity, even though we did not all fish. Dad and I did the jigging, while Mom and Ina watched. Sometimes when the boat was stopped for long periods of time Mom or Ina got seasick, especially on those days when a gentle swell caused the boat to pitch and roll in a monotonous rhythm. Whenever anyone became seasick, fishing ceased for the day and we returned to the landing. After all, Mom would have to be mobile when we reached the shore because she would still be required to serve as signal person during the hauling of the boat.

We preserved the cod using the same technique developed by Portuguese fisherman hundreds of years before. After the fish were cured, the only other thing needed for preservation was a dry storage place. No freezing or canning was necessary. The method was quite involved, and could require several weeks to complete, depending on the weather.

The fish were hoisted out of the boat with the boom and winch. We hauled the boat up, then rolled up our sleeves and began the messy job of cleaning our catch. First, Dad partially cut off the head and slit open the belly to remove the guts. Then he snapped off the head, removed the front half of the backbone, and partially severed the tail section of the fish. This allowed the fish to be spread open like a book, white meat on the face and skin and fins on the back. Next, he tossed the fish into a wooden barrel of salt water. Mom and I stood waiting by this barrel, ready to scrub off the blood and other residue. After one more quick scrubbing, the fish were ready to be salted.

Dad preferred to use the method known as dry salting. The fish were salted individually and placed one on top of the other on a flat surface. As the salt replaced the water in the fish, the resulting pickle would run off, leaving the fish relatively dry. After our day's catch was salted, it was time to head home and leave the fish to set for about four days.

A day of sunshine and low humidity was important to the final phase. When such a day came, the fish were scrubbed one last time to remove excess salt. Then we loaded them on the tractor and took them home. We had constructed a fish flake, on which to spread the fish to dry, on the side of the workshop. The flake was built using narrow spruce poles about two inches in diameter and spaced about four inches apart. If the weather remained favourable, the wind and the sun would dry the fish in about eight to ten days. In the meantime, we would have to turn them over each day at noon, carry them in at night, and cover them with a tarpaulin whenever a rain shower occurred. Finally, when they became stiff and hard and resembled wedge-shaped boards, they were dry enough to store away for winter. The finished product is known as "bacala," but we simply called it "dry fish."

My mother knew how to prepare dry codfish to make us a tasty entree on a cold winter evening. Mom would soak the hard fish in water overnight, to soften it and to remove some of the salt. Next, she would let it simmer on the stove until it was cooked. She served it with boiled potatoes, fried pork, and onions. It was truly a meal fit for royalty.

We ate a very limited amount of fresh fish during the winter because we didn't have a freezer. We ate our fill of fresh fish between May and November, when, anytime we developed an appetite for such a treat, it was just a matter of going off in the boat and jigging a cod or a couple of mackerel.

Dad's favourite species of fish, the swordfish, would always elude us. It was unlikely that we would ever encounter a swordfish, but we were always prepared. We kept the necessary equipment on board our boat at all times, since it occupied very little space.

Commercial swordfishing vessels were equipped with tall spars and specialized rigging, but on our boat we carried only the bare necessities. This included a pole, a harpoon dart, and a coil of rope. The pole was simply a large wooden dowel about twelve feet in length and less than two inches in diameter. A steel rod, the "iron," protruded from the end of the pole. This device, resembling a large hypodermic needle, was used only to insert the harpoon dart into the flesh of the swordfish.

The harpoon dart is the most critical component of the operation. The unit is made of bronze, and is designed with a socket in the rear that permits it to slip securely but loosely over the end of the iron in the pole. About a hundred fathoms (six hundred feet) of rope is attached to the dart, runs along the length of the pole, and is tucked through a tension device near the end. The rope continues on to a box, where it is coiled neatly and placed in an unrestricted area.

After a swordfish has been harpooned, the iron will slip out of the fish, leaving the dart inside as the pole floats back to the surface. As the fish speeds away, the strain on the rope causes the curved dart to back up slightly and turn crosswise inside the fish. The coil of rope spins rapidly out of the box as the fish dives deep in an effort to escape. Eventually the rope stops running out, and it is time to drown the swordfish. This is done by maintaining a gentle but firm strain on the rope. Usually it requires a couple of hours of working the rope before the fish finally dies and can be pulled to the surface. The drowning process can take only a few minutes, or it may require as much as eight hours, depending upon the location of the dart in the fish.

Whether we were cod jigging, tending the fishing net, or just out for a cruise in the boat, Dad always kept a watchful eye for swordfish. But when we finally saw one, he was caught off guard.

One late summer afternoon we were motoring along the coast beneath some high cliffs, en route to the Northeast. Suddenly a swordfish emerged from the darkened waters. Swordfish are rarely seen in September and seldom close to shore. Dad saw him first, just two points, the tip of the dorsal fin and the tail, slicing through the water ahead of the boat.

"Swordfish!" he yelled. Then he grabbed the pole and ran toward the bow.

"Edith," he barked, "get back in the stern and run the outboard."

Mom had operated the motor on previous occasions without any difficulties, but never had she been called upon to perform under such intense pressure or excitement. Dad positioned himself at the bow, where he stood poised with the harpoon firmly gripped in his hands.

"Edith," he said, "steer the boat in the direction I'm pointing the pole and listen for my instructions."

Mom looked around nervously, the look of uncertainty on her face suggesting she could be easily confused.

All our pulses quickened with anticipation. I watched carefully as we slowly approached the target. The fish seemed unaware of our presence as he swam lazily along. The movement of his fins rippled the surface of the calm water, creating a miniature wake, which was sometimes easier to see than the fins. I wondered how near the fish would permit us to come before fleeing to the safety of the depths. A swordfisherman can usually sense when a fish is about to dive. Often a "sticker" has to throw the pole some distance in order to spear the fish, while other times it can be accomplished while maintaining a grip on the harpoon. Dad was watching keenly.

We were less than sixty feet away when Dad sensed that the fish was becoming nervous. Feeling the need to increase the speed to full throttle, he turned to Mom again and screamed, "Edith, open her wide open – now!"

After a couple of seconds had elapsed without any apparent change in engine noise or speed, he yelled again, "Fast, Edith, fast!"

Suddenly, the engine went silent. The boat coasted to a stop. The swordfish swam across our bow, just beyond harpoon range, and slid beneath the water, never to be seen again.

Somehow I knew it was not engine failure that had ended the chase. I turned toward the stern. Mom was staring blindly into space, still holding onto the throttle. Guiltily, she turned to Dad and spoke in a voice that was soft and low.

"Freddy," she said, "I got mixed up and turned the handle the wrong way. I'm sorry – I turned it to 'stop' instead of 'fast'."

Dad's response was neither soft nor low, and what he said I cannot repeat. The air in the boat turned blue, matching the colour of his face. During the next few minutes he stood up and yelled a lot; then he sat down and grumbled a little. Mom kept uttering a series of excuses, which nobody listened to nor cared about. It resembled a scene from the movie *Mutiny on the Bounty*. I trusted that Dad would not do as Captain Bligh, and force my mother to "walk the plank" or be "keel-hauled."

Eventually, peace was restored on board. Mom returned to her former seat vowing never again to take the controls. She sat there dejectedly, burdened with the responsibility of losing the big one. She was unaware that before the day ended, she would have the last laugh.

Dad always said that if there was one swordfish in the area, there were likely more. Before we began the search for another fish, it was necessary to fill the position that Mom had abandoned. I was immediately promoted to helmsman and took control of the outboard. Dad stood at the bow, scanning the sea for a glimpse of another fin. Ina and Mom sat midships, quietly chatting.

I responded immediately and precisely to each command from my father, but I lacked enthusiasm. This was the third summer we had spent on St. Paul Island, and the first time we had ever seen a swordfish. In my mind, I calculated the odds of the likelihood of seeing another one on the same day. We cruised along for another hour.

Suddenly, to my disbelief, I heard my father yell that same word again: "Swordfish!" He grabbed the pole and pointed it toward the fish. I turned the boat. We were in hot pursuit, getting a chance to remedy Mom's mistake. This time, when Dad called for full power, the motor roared to life as I rotated the throttle to the "fast" position. Within a few seconds, the fish was within harpooning range.

My father took careful aim and forcefully threw the pole. I saw the harpoon stop suddenly and realized he had struck the target. As the swordfish swam past the boat in a swift descent, I could clearly see that the iron had penetrated deep into its back. This meant that the dart was set well into the fish, and would lock in that position soon after the harpoon floated out. The rope was spinning off the large coil with increasing speed as the fish accelerated and dove deeper.

Dad said that it appeared to be a relatively small swordfish, only about two hundred pounds. Just the right size for us. Some of it could be canned, some frozen, and the rest shared with the people on the Northeast. I was certain there would be fried swordfish steak for dinner.

While our mouths watered for this delicious treat, I saw the first indication that this fish might not be coming to dinner. The rope stopped running out much too soon. When Dad gave a quick tug on the rope he discovered that it had gone slack. It was obvious that another one had escaped and we wondered how that could be, as we stood there staring at each other in disbelief.

In a few minutes, the answer floated to the surface. The pole lay there on the water, the dart still firmly attached to the iron.

"That's impossible," Dad sputtered as he pulled the pole into the boat.

Careful examination revealed that the dart was so solidly attached to the iron that it required two pairs of pliers to twist it off. The bronze dart had been on the iron for a long time waiting for the fish that never came. Dad must have forgotten that when different metals are placed together, they corrode each other when not regularly lubricated, especially near salt water. Therefore, when the pole came out of the fish, it took the dart with it.

There was no yelling in the boat after this mishap. Silence filled the air. Mom could have jumped to her feet and shouted, "Freddy, a good fisherman always maintains his equipment in proper working order."

But she didn't. The consequences of such a crticism would have been serious under the best of circumstances. Instead, she pretended to sympathize with him. Dad remained in the bow, where he whimpered or mumbled from time to time.

The station logbook on that date told only half of the story. Under the "remarks" section, Dad wrote these words: "Nearly got a swordfish today. Had a poor skipper – didn't steer straight and shut off motor." There was no mention of any encounter with a second swordfish. This was a wise omission by my father, for had he told the truth about what happened the second time, he would have stolen the thunder from the first part.

Excitement of fishing, combined with the fun of boating, occupied much of the summer, but back at the station there was still work to be done. Maintenance of the station structures was a major part of my father's job. Each year Dad selected one or more of the buildings for painting. Except for the outside walls of the dwelling house, which were white, everything was painted red (in accordance with government regulations). All roofs were dark red while the walls were bright red.

Hence, much of the summer was spent with paintbrush in hand. The whole family participated in the exterior painting. Ina got more on herself than on the wall. She and I also had the responsibility of cleaning the brushes every day. Each morning we took a bucket of kerosene out in the yard and found some large rocks. We dipped the brushes in the kerosene, and then swiped them across the rocks to clean them. Within a week of our starting painting, every rock around the station was smeared with several coats of red paint.

If there was anything I despised more than handling coal, it was painting. We worked for days on buildings that always seemed to have one more wall left to paint. I found it a welcome change to take a break from the painting now and then and tend to codfish drying on the flake. The painting would have gone much faster had we been familiar with, or even known about, using rollers with long handles for outside painting. Instead, we used paintbrushes and ladders until the job was finally done. It always seemed just when I thought the last lick of paint had been applied, Dad would say, "Well, Edith, I think it needs another coat!"

No one could be expected to spend the entire summer working at the light station or catching and curing our winter supply of cod. We often took a day off and went to one of the beaches, where we would have a wiener roast or a picnic. I was unable to take full advantage of the beach, since I couldn't swim. I wouldn't learn how on St. Paul, either. The beach and shallows were carpeted with large, slippery boulders, making it very difficult to even wade for a few moments without falling over. Aside from that, the water was extremely cold. Those agile and brave enough to wade soon learned that the bottom dropped off very quickly, making swimming skills suddenly very necessary. I could only stand on the shore and imagine the thrill of diving into the crystal clear water.

However, there were two locations on the island where it was safe to play in the water. Two relatively large freshwater lakes high above sea level are nestled in the center of the island. The lakes are similar, not only in size, but also in shape, and each lake covers an area of approximately eighty acres. They differ only in depth. The southern lake, Lake Lena, is so shallow that during the summer months, lily pads cover its entire surface. Lake Ethel, which is much deeper, lies about half a mile away in the northern part of the island. Each lake is surrounded by a growth of dense spruce trees.

Petrie's Point and the site of the New Brunswick lifesaving station. Lake Lena is in the background. (Billy Budge photo)

Previous island dwellers had maintained a walking path from Atlantic Cove to both lakes. We explored each lake but chose the shallow one for most of our outings. On the shore of Lake Lena, someone had partially constructed a log cabin. One of the radio operators had undertaken this project while suffering from the St. Paul equivalent of the northern complaint known as "cabin fever." Nevertheless, it provided Ina and I with a place to play, while our parents relaxed in the shade or prepared a picnic.

One day while wading in the lake, we came upon something that provided even more entertainment. The same individual who worked on the cabin must also have constructed a boat. It was lying on the bottom in about two feet of water, and with a little help from Dad, we pulled it on shore. The primitive construction suggested it was probably built on location with limited tools. The simple design featured a box shape with straight sides and square ends. There were several large holes in the bottom where a number of the boards had split. I felt that, with a little work and imagination, this boat could be made seaworthy again.

On the next visit to the lake, we came prepared to make minor repairs to the boat. We nailed lobster pot lathes and tarpaper over the cracks in the boards. It was patched on both the inside and the outside, somewhat resembling a re-floated shipwreck out of one of my favourite books: *Scuppers the Sailor Man*. The repair job took care of most of the leaks, and regular bailing kept the boat relatively dry. Using a set of oars that Dad borrowed from our other boat, Ina and I spent many hours rowing that old boat around the lake.

Summer boating on Lake Lena. (Edith Budge photo)

Dad heard a rumour that neither lake contained any fish, and we made no effort to prove otherwise. My father was quite content to take that person at their word. He had no luck or patience fishing in lakes, even on the mainland where he knew trout lived in abundance. If there were no trout present in the lake, there was at least one form of aquatic life. Ina and I often saw very small eel-like "fish" swimming in the water near the shore, but could not identify the species. Many years later I learned that these were probably very large leeches.

When the last flowers of summer had faded away and the cool breezes of autumn whispered a prelude for the season ahead, we knew it was time for the final harvest. Mom planted a small garden near our house, but there was little to be reaped. A few carrots and radishes struggled to grow in about four inches of soil on top of the bedrock. However, on a windswept hillside, nature had worked alone all summer to produce the greatest crop of all: cranberries. Early fall was picking time.

Just north of Lake Ethel, a grassy area nearly cuts the island in two. The field, known as Martin Powers, sits like a green saddle across the isthmus, steeply sloped on both sides and gently rounded over the top. At the foot of the slopes on either side, the field drops away to vertical cliffs and into the sea.

Cranberries thrive on boggy soil, where they grow thick in scores of small patches. There is a striking difference in the colour of the berries found in different sections of the slope. We found that many of the berries were brown-speckled, while in other areas they were almost blue, and, of course, there was the more common red colour. They tasted the same even though they looked vastly different.

We left the farm tractor parked behind the vacant structures of the wireless station when picking time came. This was the end of the road. From here we continued on foot, following the trail toward the Northeast. About halfway along that trail, the road comes out at Martin Powers. Here Dad would remove his backpack and pull out a white pillowcase. Holding it up, he'd announce, "When this is filled we can all go home."

It seemed like a tall order to have to fill such a large container, but everyone began picking with great enthusiasm.

About two hours after the task had begun, enthusiasm would begin to wane. Ina would be the first, wandering around more and picking less until she finally quit. Long after Ina had given up, I would still feel determined to pick until the job was done. But before long, monotony and boredom would take their toll, causing my best intentions to slowly unravel. By late afternoon, my parents were left to fill the sack alone. When it was finally filled, Dad placed the bag into his backpack and we were homeward bound. Leading the way, Dad stomped heavily down the trail, spurred on by the weight of more than nine gallons of cranberries on his back. We returned many times before the season ended to pick berries at Martin Powers.

Once home, the berries were poured into a large box to await the final task. We had picked the cranberries out of the grass, but at home, we picked the grass out of the cranberries. When time came to clean them, Dad pulled out the large box of berries from their storage place and into the middle of the kitchen floor. Each of us took positions around the box, like cubs sitting around a campfire. By slowly cleaning one handful at a time, the straw, the leaves, and the rotten berries would be discarded, leaving only clean ripened berries for cooking.

This would have been a boring and time-consuming ordeal had it not been for Dad's storytelling. He often spun yarns about some of the old folks back home, telling funny tales of things they had said and done. Sometimes, we all sang country songs like "Railroad Steamboat" by Jim Reeves and "Wake Up, Little Suzie" by the Everly Brothers. The radio provided the necessary entertainment when no one was interested in singing or talking. In this manner, the long evenings of cleaning berries passed quickly, and what seemed to be an impossible task was suddenly finished.

My mother did all the preserving, working alone with her secret recipe. She stewed the berries on the stovetop, using one large pot at a time. In the cellar, the shelves began to sag under the weight of countless bottles of cranberry jam. Mom was completing the final jars of preserves when nature was painting the last days of summer. Outside, the early morning frost covered the golden grass and lingered on the bushes, ushering in a new season.

10

Fire!

My father was not a lamplighter, but a lightkeeper. There was much more involved in keeping the light operational than in just lighting it. Throughout the night, a constant watch was kept to ensure that the light continued to burn brightly and that the lens assembly rotated properly around it. That didn't mean the lightkeeper sat constantly in front of the window, one hand on his knee and the other under his chin, posed like Auguste Rodin's sculpture "The Thinker," waiting for the light to go out. A quick glance through the window about every thirty minutes was usually enough. Early detection of a malfunction was very important; this would give the lightkeeper ample time to correct the situation before it got out of control.

Once the light was activated, Dad would often spend the next few hours relaxing in his favourite chair, listening to the radio while the rest of us kept an eye on the lighthouse. It required little effort on my part to lift my head from schoolwork now and again to cast a glance through the window toward the lighthouse. Mom did likewise whenever she passed the window doing her housework. This gave my father a welcome break during the early evening hours prior to bedtime. After that, he would be left alone to keep the light burning until daylight.

Even though we were checking frequently, Dad was still concerned that we might miss the first sign of trouble. During the course of the evening, he frequently repeated his favourite line, "Would someone check the light and make sure it's not jumping up and down?"

Normally, a bright white light equal to several hundred watts was emitted from the mantle behind the lens. If there was an obstruction in the fuel line or a loss of air pressure, the white light changed into a yellow ball of flame that engulfed the mantle as well as the apparatus beneath it. We saw the fire reflected through the prisms of the lens, and it would appear to be hopping when this malfunction was viewed from our house.

Dad stood up in the early hours of one cold January morning and approached the window for a routine check. What he saw was unbelievable. He quickly wiped the window with his hand, thinking that perhaps the frost on the glass had created an illusion. A second look confirmed that the scene was real, and this time it was not only the mantle that was on fire. Flames were dancing all over the upper level of the lighthouse, casting only an eerie yellow glow through the large windows.

Dad donned his winter apparel and rushed out the door. He knew that the lighthouse itself would not be destroyed, since it was constructed from steel and concrete, but the fire could cause major damage to the equipment. He also knew it could only be the kerosene fuel that was burning, since there were no other combustible materials present. To extinguish the fire he would have to reach the fuel supply valve and turn it off. This might prove to be a difficult and dangerous task. The valve was not located near the access hatch where it could easily be reached from the top of the ladder. Dad would be forced to directly enter the area of flames and walk around to the other side of the equipment to reach the valve.

As my father raced up the pathway toward the lighthouse, he recalled how the light had been lit earlier that evening and the duties he had performed to ensure its continuous operation. If the mishap had been caused by his own hand, he would be responsible for the damages, and could lose his job. Had he become too complacent with this mundane task, and failed to check some important item vital to proper performance and safety? Like a video machine in fast-forward mode, his mind raced through the sequence of steps that he completed each time he lit the light, thus reassuring himself that he had not made an error. The complexity of the job required careful attention to every detail.

With only one exception, everything pertaining to the operation of the light was located on the top floor, known as the lantern of the lighthouse. A steel ladder permanently secured between the bottom and top floor provided the only access to the lantern's equipment. After reaching the top of the ladder, you entered the lantern through a hole in the floor. Once inside the lantern, a steel hatch cover was lowered over the opening, making it possible to safely walk around and service all of the various components of the light.

In one section, two small tanks stood side by side. The smaller one was filled with kerosene while the larger tank was pressurized with air. A hand pump, similar to a car tire pump, was positioned between the tanks. It was made of brass, and since it was bolted to the floor, it was unnecessary to hold one foot on the base during the pumping operation.

The working pressure for the light was forty pounds per square inch and required about twenty minutes of pumping to accomplish. My father usually performed this part of the operation as I was too small to push down the handle easily, especially after air pressure began to increase. Lack of air pressure could cause a malfunction, but my father remembered checking the gauge after ignition that evening. It had read forty pounds of pressure, just as it should.

The light, as well as the revolving lens assembly, sat on top of a steel stand secured to a concrete pedestal in the centre of the floor. The lens apparatus weighed several hundred pounds and measured more than two feet in height. It was shaped like an egg, mounted vertically, and flattened on the top and bottom, thus giving it a diameter about equal to its height. A brass framework held the prisms and lenses together in this hollow glass sphere. The magnifying lenses were located in the centre of the sphere and were spaced at unequal intervals around the circumference.

To a distant ship, the light appeared to be flashing on and off. Really, this was an illusion produced as each lens rotated past the fixed light. Up close, the light never seemed to flash off. Its reflection through the window danced on our living room wall like a flickering campfire.

The unequal time between each flash, made possible by the uneven spacing of the lenses, sent out a specified flash sequence code. Each lighthouse had a unique flash code by which it was identified. The series of curved prisms positioned around each

A Fresnel lens similar to the one in the Southwest Light. (Billy Budge photo)

lens served to intensify the light. This intricate assembly of lenses and prisms is known as a Fresnel lens. My father's greatest concern was that if the fire was not extinguished in its early stages, the glass could fracture or fall out of the frame due to the excessive heat.

One section of the Fresnel lens was actually a door that swung open, providing access to the light inside. The light itself consisted of a small venturi tube mounted vertically in a metal bowl. A mantle similar to that used on a gas lantern was attached to the top of the tube. One end of the fuel line was attached to the base of the tube while the other end was connected to the tanks on the floor.

Once the fuel tank was filled and the pressurized air tank pumped up, the light was ready to be lit. Before this could be done the venturi tube would have to be preheated. To accomplish this, the metal bowl was filled with alcohol, and this ignited with a match. While the alcohol flames were heating the tube, Dad used a special pin to clean out the tiny orifice in the top of the tube where the hot kerosene vapour would enter the mantle.

This was a very important cleaning, because it required only a small speck of dirt to obstruct the fine spray of fuel. Such a blockage would cause raw kerosene to run out through the tiny opening, pour down onto the base, or the floor, where it would burn out of control. A similar malfunction probably destroyed the previous lighthouse in 1916. That fire not only destroyed the wooden lighthouse, but also levelled the lightkeeper's dwelling house right next door.

After the cleaning was complete and the small flame had licked away the last drop of alcohol, it was finally time for ignition. The first step was to quickly open the fuel supply valve which sent pressurized kerosene up through the preheated tube. Dad then stepped up on the concrete pedestal, where he greeted this very flammable vapour with a lit match held just above the mantle. In an instant, the mantle caught and was burning. The mantle was probably meant to be self-igniting, and probably was at one time, but all the time my father was lightkeeper he had to coax it to life using an introduced flame.

While my father was working through the various procedures involved in the lighting, I would be preparing it for rotation. The flashing or rotation was made possible by heavy weights pulling on a geared mechanism located just below the Fresnel lens. Outside the lighthouse these weights were attached to a carriage that was suspended from a steel messenger cable. One end of this fixed cable was attached to the lighthouse, while the other end was anchored in the rock about fifty feet below the base of the lighthouse. The power generated by the force of these weights rolling down the cable kept the lens rotating throughout the night.

Each evening at the time of lighting, it was my job to crank up the weights, using a hand winch that was built into the mechanism. This task could be referred to as "winding up" the lens, in much the same way that folks used to wind up their alarm clocks.

In the summer this was a relatively easy chore, because the brief period of darkness did not permit the carriage to travel very far down the cable before the light was extinguished at daybreak. During the long winter nights, however, not only did the weights run nearly all the way to the bottom, but Dad added several more weights for extra pressure against ice and snow that might accumulate on the suspension cable. During these months of heavy cranking, I would be forced to rest several times before the weights were finally up.

Once the light was lit, I released the brake on the winch, which started the lens rotating, and the carriage slowly began to roll down the cable again. I was always amazed at the amount of force the weights applied to the rotating mechanism when it required little more than the touch of one's finger on the lens to stop it from rotating.

Freezing rain was the worst kind of weather to face. Often Dad was left to deal with this by himself while the rest of us slept. The light had to be watched very closely at such times because the rotation would most likely stop before the weather cleared. This meant the weighted carriage had frozen to the suspension cable. When this happened, my father responded with a ladder and a hammer. He placed the ladder against the side of the ice-covered lighthouse and climbed to the top, where he would pound on the suspension cable with the hammer. The resulting vibration shook off the ice accretion and freed the carriage to travel once again. If the freezing rain continued, this procedure would have to be repeated several times before the dawn.

My father would gladly choose to work outside in foul weather with freezing temperatures, rather than face a fire on the inside. Extinguishing a fire in such a confined space carried the risk of suffering severe burns, a life-threatening situation in a place where medical help was hours or even days away. This reality caused him to proceed with caution as he opened the lighthouse door and stepped inside.

Burning chips of paint were peeling from the ceiling and falling through the hatchway. Dodging the burning debris, he hastily climbed the ladder. At the top of the ladder, he discovered that the situation was not as bad as it appeared from the outside. There were small puddles of kerosene still burning on the concrete pedestal, as well as on the lens base, but there was little flame on the floor. Carefully, he crawled around to the other side of the equipment and closed the fuel supply valve. He noticed that the air pressure in the tank was almost zero: the fire was slowly dying on its own, due to fuel starvation.

Dad extinguished the flames quickly and stepped back to survey the damage. Forty years of ceiling paint now lay in ashes on the floor. Parts of the wall and much of the equipment were also stripped of paint. Curtains of black kerosene smoke shrouded all the windows. It was the Fresnel lens that had sustained the most serious damage. The normally crystal-clear lens assembly was draped in a veil of black soot. One of the prisms had fallen out of the frame and several others were loose. Fortunately, none of the glass had broken so most of the damage was superficial.

Later the cleanup would begin, but at this time it was more important to discover the cause of the fire. Dad tested the light by relighting it in the usual manner. The problem was as he had suspected. The venturi tube was partially obstructed by a small foreign particle. Every evening the kerosene was strained through a special filter before being poured into the tank, but occasionally dirt would still pass through, only to lodge in the tube sometime later.

Being preoccupied with the fire and the mess it left behind, my father failed to notice a more serious problem. The lens that should still be rotating in spite of the fire was standing motionless in front of him. He soon discovered that tiny bits of burnt paint had fallen in between the base of the lens assembly and the housing in which it rotated. This debris had been wedged into position by the force of the rotation, and all movement had ceased. Dad realized that it would be impossible to remove these foreign particles without taking the lens assembly apart. The gap between the two surfaces was very narrow, and the housing was about ten inches deep, too awkward to get into with a hand or even a tool. He would need technical help to deal with this problem.

It was almost daylight when Dad finally left the lighthouse. Immediately, he began preparing a message to be sent to the office of the Superintendent of Lighthouses in Dartmouth, Nova Scotia. The text included an official report on the mishap and briefly described the situation at the scene. He also assured the superintendent that the light would be operational that same evening but it would not be rotating. Before any attempt was made to correct that problem he would have to await instructions from the engineering division.

The following morning, over the radio telephone, Dad received a detailed message containing the necessary information on how to repair the seized apparatus. The lens would first have to be hoisted off the stand until the base was completely out of the housing. With the lens out of the way, the debris could be easily removed. Once the cleanup was completed, it was simply a matter of lowering the apparatus back into its position and reconnecting it. The solution sounded easy enough, but it would require several days of preparation before the actual lift could take place.

Work on the clean up began almost immediately, with our whole family involved. Just to be certain that he understood each and every step, Dad completed the job mentally before he began. He decided to use a tackle (a system of ropes and pulleys) for the hoist. The top pulley would be hooked into the metal ring in the centre of the ceiling. Scores of metal rods fanned outward from this ring, each terminating against the circular wall of the lighthouse. It resembled the spokes in a wheel, with the ring serving as the hub.

The lantern of the Southwest Light.

The only problem was that the ring was basically unsupported. Any attempt to use it as an anchor to raise the massive lens would result in pulling down the ring with all the spokes. Therefore, in accordance with the engineer's instructions, we started bracing each individual spoke from the floor.

Mom and I began dragging heavy wooden planks out of the workshop and up the path to the lighthouse. There Dad cut each one to the exact length necessary to reach from the floor to the ceiling. Then we began the slow task of positioning and wedging each individual piece, until a forest of posts surrounded the lens. It took more than a day to complete the bracing, but finally we were ready to connect the hoist to what was now a solid, reinforced ring.

At first Dad intended to use the tractor for power, but later decided to use two double tackles connected in series. Several hours were spent weaving the ropes through all the pulleys that formed the tackle and connecting it to the lens.

Finally, Dad threw the end of the rope down to the lower floor and called on Mom to begin hoisting. She caught the rope and began to pull. It came up so easily at first that I felt she was only taking up the slack. Then Dad yelled, "It's coming up!"

At the time, I didn't understood the principle of this pulley system, where time and distance are sacrificed for power. I was quite puzzled, watching my mother rapidly pulling down such a vast amount of rope, while the lens came up so slowly that I could barely notice it moving. When the apparatus was high above the housing and safely out of the way, Mom climbed up the ladder to see for herself. The satisfaction she derived from this great accomplishment was obvious, her face beaming with pride and excitement. There was no doubt she deserved a great deal of respect for her participation, because, according to the engineers, the lens assembly weighed 750 pounds, and my 100-pound mother had lifted it by herself.

My father suggested that perhaps Ina and I would like to clean out the housing. He passed me a small piece of glass for scraping away the debris. We eagerly agreed to do our part, oblivious to the dangerous environment in which we were about to work. Soon after I began to scrape, I noticed that the bottom of the housing was covered with a molten, lead-like substance. Ina and I became quite interested in this strange material and wondered what it was. Dad, who was unaware that this was a very toxic element, showed little interest in our fascination, saying, "The stuff is only mercury!"

The housing was actually nothing more than a large bowl of mercury that provided both flotation and lubrication for the lens.

It was only when I accidentally dropped my piece of glass into the solution that I noticed one of the unique characteristics of this peculiar metal. We were both shocked to see the glass floating on top of the mercury, like a cork floating on water. This inspired Ina to experiment with a wrench, only to find that it also floated high in the mercury. When a piece of lead dropped in gave the same results, I made the erroneous conclusion that nothing will sink in mercury. However, I am told by sci-entists that gold and platinum will sink in it.

With the cleaning and experimenting completed, Ina and I decided to play while our parents continued to scrub and polish other equip-ment. We loaded up wrenches with nuts and bolts, and sailed them back and forth in the vat of mercury. Sometimes we placed our hands in this strange liquid, to support our weight when we reached across to the other side, and marvelled at how they never got wet. We spent the rest of the afternoon sailing imaginary boats of solid steel across a silver sea of mercury. Dad ended all the fun when he lowered the lens back into its previous position and filled in our playground. When we all left the lighthouse that evening it was both shining and rotating, sweeping its bright beams of light far across a lonely sea.

That night at dinner we had two reasons to celebrate. First of all, the light that had been standing still for four days was finally rotating and, therefore, flashing again. It was made possible by Dad's determi-nation to get the job done and the whole family pulling together (except for Mom, who pulled alone!).

Secondly, it was my birthday. Somehow, amid her regular house-work and the long hours spent working at the lighthouse, Mom had found the time to bake a cake complete with ten candles and fancy decorations. My birthday present was a small radio receiver kit that had been stashed away months before for this occasion. After the trio had sung "Happy Birthday," we all retired to the living room for a well-deserved rest. While the others listened to the radio, I spent the evening working on my new receiver.

11

The Duck Hunter Blues

There were times when simple complaining was sufficient to bring about a desired change. But for those times when Lady Luck dealt us a miserable hand, only determination and perseverance kept us in the game. The game that would become the greatest challenge was duck hunting. Although Dad never blamed me for any of the hunting problems we encountered, I could not deny that I was responsible for many of them.

In the beginning, I was happy hunting with my new .22 calibre rifle. For an eight-year-old, such killing capability should have been more than adequate. But somehow it never seemed fair. Dad and I suffered an equal amount from wind and cold while we watched and waited patiently for the ducks to come in close enough for us to shoot.

Mostly, it was Dad who watched and I waited. I often stared blindly in the same direction as my father as he watched the movements of each flock. Standing beside him, I would strain my eyes in a desperate attempt to see the ducks, but I could discern nothing but ocean. I didn't know at the time, but I was shortsighted and needed glasses. My father never recognized my handicap and his lack of patience with me made matters worse.

As he carefully studied the movements of the invisible flock, I sat shivering and waiting for him to say those welcome words, "They're swimming in." Then I knew that soon I would see them, too. At times the long waits in the bitter cold gave me such great discomfort that finally, with teeth chattering, I had to ask, "Dad, where are they at now?" His loud, gravelly voice blasted a response that varied little each time I asked: "They're just outside that rock. Billy, I can't believe you're that stupid you can't see those birds!"

Me at age eight, with two ducks I shot with my .22.

"I can see them," I would say, calming him down, even though I couldn't.

By virtue of his more deadly weapon, Dad claimed the privilege of the first shot. His single-shot 12-gauge shotgun could blast a spray of lead across the water, often leaving two or three ducks dead.

Then it was my turn to shoot. Even though they were sitting ducks, the shot was not an easy one. The surviving birds, made nervous by the shotgun blast, prepared to fly. Their bodies sank low into the water. Only their slender necks and tiny heads, speeding through the water, were visible. At the same time, the ducks were bobbing on the waves. Since my rifle fired only a single bullet, I would take careful aim and fire. Sometimes I got lucky, but most of the time I missed.

At the end of the day, my father led the way home bearing his prize of two or three ducks while I trudged along behind him, usually empty-handed. This scene was happening all too often. I felt that there was a need for change.

Complaining worked to get me the .22, so one night after dinner (when it appeared that my father was in the proper mood) I complained again.

"Dad," I began, "I appreciate the .22 calibre rifle you bought me last year, but now I would really like to have a shotgun."

Dad responded by saying, "No, Billy, I'm afraid not. The kick [recoil] from a 12-gauge shotgun would be too much for you to stand."

However, he felt that perhaps a smaller size shotgun would be the answer. He promised me that I would have one for the next hunting season.

When the supply ship arrived the following September, I was there to meet it, as usual, but with even much more enthusiasm than normal. I watched the sling-loads of supplies as they came up and carefully scrutinized each package. When I spied a long, narrow cardboard box being placed on the grass I rushed over and picked it up. After Dad agreed that this was probably it, I tore open the package and removed a shiny new 410-gauge shotgun.

Mom didn't share much of my excitement. She was always afraid of guns, especially a shotgun wielded by an eight-year-old child. But my father had taught me about the danger of guns; together, we were a safety-conscious family with regard to firearms. Mom would constantly remind me it was always an "empty" gun that accidentally discharged and killed someone. For that reason, no loaded firearms were ever kept inside the house. Our guns weren't even loaded outside until we were in a shooting position, and only then at the last possible moment.

With a full understanding of the importance of safety, I went outside with Dad where he taught me how to properly handle and use a shotgun. The target was nothing more than an empty milk can, which he placed on a fence post. Before I pulled the trigger, he cautioned me to hold the gun firmly against my shoulder in order to minimize the kick. The gun blasted, the can flew off the post, but I withstood the recoil easily. When I saw the can, peppered with holes, lying in the grass, I knew from now on the ducks were in deep trouble.

That autumn, I felt somewhat more mature when I went off hunting with a shotgun instead of the lowly .22. It wasn't long before I shot my first duck and was looking forward to shooting many more as the season progressed. There was no doubt that the new gun was a vast improvement. I did have more luck than the previous year, but there were times when I still came up short.

The 410-gauge is the smallest of all shotguns and herein lies the problem. Since the effective range of the 410 is considerably less than that of the 12-gauge, the birds would have to be quite near the shore before I could shoot. Many times Dad would turn to me and say, "Billy, these birds are too far away for your gun, and there's no need to waste your shells firing at them." At such times it would have been better that I still had the rifle because at least I could have had the pleasure of participating in the action.

Even though I never complained when this situation arose, Dad must have sensed my displeasure. One afternoon, when we were sitting outside, Dad asked me if I would like to try a shot with his 12-gauge. I accepted the offer and ran for his gun while he placed another can on the fencepost. I blasted as before with much the same results, except that this time the recoil was much more powerful. Even though it shook me up a little, it didn't bruise my shoulder nor did I lose control of the gun. When he saw that I could safely handle the 12-gauge, he came up to me and said, "The gun is yours!" I had no idea what he was going to use himself; what I did know was that I was nine years old and had at last become a man.

After he made the presentation, he turned away and walked toward the workshop. I followed him inside where I watched him pull down from the rafters a long wooden box. He began removing what looked like a rusty piece of pipe. Then I saw that it was in fact an old single shot 12-gauge shotgun. When Dad rubbed his hand along the barrel, flakes of rust fell off and accumulated on the floor. It had an odd-shaped stock that was weathered and cracked. Any finish it might have had, had long since disappeared. With a lot of work it might have been made presentable as an antique, but I failed to understand how he could still use it for its intended purpose. Dad said that the gun had been left to him by my great-grandfather, and there was some doubt as to whether or not he was the original owner.

According to my father, it was still operable; all that it needed was a little cleaning. He picked up a piece of sandpaper, and the rust and dust began to fly. A few hours later the white steel of the barrel began to show through, except in the deep pits where the rust would remain. Dad even sanded a little of the stock, exposing some fresh wood and making the grain visible in a few places. Then, using a paint brush and a can of regular black paint, he painted the barrel and all the other metal parts. To my dismay, he also painted the wooden stock black. After giving it a dab of oil here and there, it was finally ready for action. The finished product resembled a gun, especially if viewed from a distance.

The next time we went hunting, there was equality between us and no longer would I have any excuses for my failures. When my father felt that the birds were within range, we would both fire together and reap the rewards. It was a pleasure to hunt with the proper equipment and I was happy.

My father, on the other hand, was becoming increasingly annoyed with his weapon. It developed a tendency to come apart at the most inopportune times. Quite often when he fired, the explosion caused the gun to disassemble, leaving him holding only the stock and forearm in his hand. The barrel quickly departed the scene, tumbling down over the rocks until it finally come to rest in the nearest crevice. Before he could fire off a second round, he would have to gather up the parts, reassemble, and reload. Indeed, this gun gave new meaning to the term "single shot." Even after he taped the gun together with black friction tape, the separations continued to occur from time to time.

My father's patience was constantly being tested by this unsafe and defective firearm, but one particular incident tempted him to heave it into the sea. When he tried to fire on a sure target, in a situation where the duck was as good as dead, the gun refused to fire. He repeatedly cocked the hammer and pulled the trigger but the only sound from the gun was a soft click. By the time we left for home, Dad had deduced that the problem was a broken firing pin.

Back at the workshop, he disassembled the firing mechanism. In no time at all the broken pin was removed and we both carefully examined the defective part. I suggested that we try making a firing pin, using a stove bolt. When Dad found one approximately the right size, he placed it in the vice and we began to file. While we worked we joked about how easy it should be to create the part. We agreed that all we had to do was to keep filing the bolt until we had cut away everything that didn't look like a firing pin. It took us the entire afternoon to make the part, but before it was time to attend to the lighthouse Dad had the gun reassembled.

He should have tested it before we went out into the field but my father wasn't one to waste ammunition. I was quite sceptical about the repair job, but the first time we encountered a flock of ducks Dad squeezed the trigger and the gun blasted off its round. When the smoke cleared he turned to me and proudly said, "See, Billy, I told you it would work." However, when he tried to reload the gun, it wouldn't open. He even tried breaking it open across his knee while he pressed on the release lever, but it stayed firmly shut.

It was a very difficult job to make such precision parts with primitive equipment and material: we had made a slight error. The firing pin is designed to strike the cap in the centre of the cartridge with just enough force to dent it, causing a spark which sets off the charge. Then the pin retracts back into its housing. We had made the firing pin a little too long, causing the hammer to drive the pin deep into the cartridge, where it lodged. Dad's gun was, in effect, nailed together. After we finally got it open, we made a slight modification with the file and all was well again.

One chilly morning in early December, fate placed us in the right place at the right time. We had wasted most of a day waiting in the cold out on Petrie's Point without getting an opportunity to shoot anything. Suddenly, a large flock of Common Eider ducks came flapping past. They were closely grouped, half-flying and half-running over the water. Dad fired and several birds dropped together. I fired at almost the same time with similar results. For the next few minutes we continued shooting at the wounded and confused survivors, until finally twelve birds lay dead on the water. Never before had we killed so many ducks in a single day, nor would we ever do it again.

Having to deal with so many birds at one time presented us with some problems. Most of the time, we killed only two or three ducks a week. We plucked, singed, and cleaned them in the workshop. We used a blowtorch to burn or singe the remaining feathers or down off the skin.

Twelve ducks made a sizeable pile on the workshop floor. Neither Dad nor myself was much enthused about sitting in that cold, unheated building picking ducks for several hours. Dad thought about it for a moment and said, "Maybe, for this one time, Mom will let us pick them in the kitchen." She agreed saying, "I think that's a good idea but you guys will have to be careful. I don't want feathers flying all through my house."

It was a pleasure to sit beside the kitchen stove, each of us with a duck across one knee and a cardboard box between us to catch the feathers. Picking is not a difficult chore, and after one acquires the knack and develops a rhythm, the feathers come off fairly quickly. Dad and I were both good pickers, but with so many to do Mom suggested that she and Ina give us a hand. They each picked up a duck and we made a family circle around the box.

Mom and Ina were pitiful to watch – Mom would try to get some feathers wrapped around her finger and awkwardly jerk them out; Ina more or less pretended to pick. As the evening wore on, Ina got more and more feathers on her face, hair, and body. By bedtime, she had more on herself than she had actually picked out of the ducks. This prompted Dad to muse, "Who's going to pick Ina when we're done?"

The ensuing bursts of laughter excited the dog. He jumped into the centre of the circle, landing with all fours in the box, generating an explosion of feathers. He stood there barking, sending fluffy clouds of down throughout the house. The scene was hilarious and even Mom could not avoid laughing (though she knew that in the end she would have to clean up most of the mess).

The second problem was what to do with the ducks when they were cleaned. Mom always cooked the ducks we normally shot each week for Sunday dinner. This free, and always fresh, source of meat stretched out our limited supply of frozen beef and pork. The refrigerator was still nearly full, as we had only recently received our annual shipment of groceries. Since there was no way to freeze the ducks, (and no friends to invite over for a feast), we had to find some other method to preserve them.

I listened to my parents discussing a solution and from what I could hear, it seemed that the canned lobsters on the shelf were about to get some company. Mom did the final cleaning and scraping of the ducks, then baked them in the oven several at a time. When the cooking was complete, the canning process began. The birds were cut up, pressed into cans and, finally, sealed in their own gravy. Canned duck provided us with a fast and tasty snack on those days when my mother was too involved with other household chores to cook. It was also unique, in that it was not the sort of thing you would find on the shelf of your local supermarket.

The success of that hunting trip put me on a high that lasted for several days. The trouble with being on top of the world is there isn't anywhere else to go but down. The descent began with the discovery that we were almost out of ammunition. When my father had placed his order for 12-gauge shells, he did not know that his son would also become a 12-gauge man and help deplete his inventory. There was indeed some cause for concern when we realized that we were using the last box of shells.

Our fears were quickly relieved when Dad received a call on the radio telephone from the supply ship *Edward Cornwallis*. The ship was still in North Sydney, and the Captain wondered if there was anything that we needed. Dad responded in the affirmative and asked him to pick up six boxes of 12-gauge shells, as well as a few other items, and the mail. Once again we kept our fingers crossed and put our trust in that elusive Christmas boat.

The morning the ship dropped anchor off Atlantic Cove we had only a few rounds of ammunition left. The trail, normally soft and muddy, was frozen solid with only a dusting of snow in the bottom of the wheel ruts. Sunshine and calm water prefigured an excellent landing. The whole order came ashore packed in one cardboard box, which we tossed aboard the tractor. After thanking the crew in the lifeboat and wishing them all a merry Christmas, we motored back up the trail. I turned and looked back one last time at the shrinking image of the launch and its occupants. These men would be the last outsiders we would see for several months.

Back home, Dad set the large box on the table. I began tearing it open in a semi pre-Christmas frenzy. I was interested only in one thing but I had to remove various other items in order to reach it. The newspapers on the top were actually reading material for my father but the news it contained had by this time become history. Reading the many letters from relatives and friends would take my parents most of the day. There was some foodstuff, as well as a few last minute Christmas parcels from my grandparents.

What I saw at the bottom of the box stopped me cold. Dad, noticing the frown on my face, asked, "What's wrong, Billy?"

"It's these boxes of shot shells, Dad. They look small."

I removed one for a closer look. When I saw the writing on the box, a lather of cold sweat suddenly formed over my body. I could actually feel my shirt sticking to my skin. At the same time, a puzzled look on Dad's face indicated that he too thought something was terribly wrong. Written in bold letters on the top of each box were the words "16-GAUGE SHOT SHELLS."

I put the box on the table and just stood there gazing in disbelief. I thought that perhaps if I stared at the carton long enough, the shells would miraculously transform themselves into usable ammunition. Or maybe someone would awaken me from a terrible dream and we could continue to hunt as though nothing had happened.

Even the weather outside had suddenly changed, as if to reflect our feelings. The early morning sun had vanished. From a gloomy sky, a light snow squall swept across the island. Snowflakes were slanting across the kitchen window, and in the grey distance the departing supply ship was barely visible. By this time, the sailors on board would be enjoying their lunch, totally oblivious to the parcel of pain they had just delivered.

I held one of the cartridges in my hand for a moment, then rushed outside to see how well it would fit into the 12-gauge. I came back filled with excitement, and yelled to my father, "The shell fits very loosely into the chamber but the rim is large enough to keep it from slipping up the barrel – maybe it will work."

He suggested I give it a try. I placed a can on the fencepost we used for target practice. I pulled the trigger. The shell went off, but the explosion sounded more like a puff than a bang. There was little or no recoil. Not one single shot had penetrated the can or even dented it. Seeing that there was nothing to lose I fired a second round, with similar results. So very weak was the blast, I felt certain that had I not tilted the gun forward, the shot would have remained inside the barrel.

When we examined the two empty 16-gauge cartridges it became clear why this substitution would not work. Each shell casing had split along its entire length. We concluded that the main force of the burning powder was expended by enlarging the shell casing to fit the chamber instead of discharging the load of shot. It was obvious why one required the proper ammunition. Now what I really wanted for Christmas was a 16-gauge shotgun to fit these shells!

Suddenly, my father said that he had an idea that might resolve the dilemma. He pulled a small wooden box down from a shelf in the workshop. The box contained the remains of a kit that he had once used to load his own ammunition. There wasn't much of it left anymore, but there were enough caps to make about fifteen rounds and a few basic tools to do the job. The containers that once held powder and lead shot were empty. These materials could be acquired by opening the 16-gauge shells and removing their contents. But first we would have to return to our more popular hunting sites in hopes of recovering a number of empty 12-gauge cartridges for reloading.

In the days that followed, I would often glance up from my school work to watch my father perform the delicate transplant operation. First, he removed the used cap from the empty shell casing and replaced it with a new one from his kit. Then he refilled it with the lead shot and powder he removed from the 16-gauge shells. The two components were separated in the casing by wads, of which there was a limited supply. Finally, he closed off the mouth of the shell by refolding the pleats at the end. Sometimes it required several hours to produce a couple of shells, and with only a few caps left in the kit, production was about to cease.

I never fired any of my father's homemade ammunition, allowing him instead to hunt alone. It was not that I didn't trust my father's shells; rather, I didn't trust myself. I had been known to miss from time to time and I was not about to waste any of the shells that he had spent so much time creating. Furthermore, by this time Dad's patience was running low and there was no doubt that I was the root cause for most of his woes. It was simply too risky for me to shoot, in the event that I might find myself in a situation where I had to kill or be killed.

It was shaping up to be a winter without any hunting, as I observed my father making up his last usable rounds. I picked up a 16-gauge shell that would remain intact since there was no longer any use for its contents. On the shelf there were five full boxes each containing twenty-five similar rounds. Somehow it didn't seem possible that we could have so much of what we needed but nothing that we could use. There had to be a way.

I wistfully toyed with the shells, unaware that I was holding the solution to our dilemma in my hands. In one hand, I held the full 16-gauge cartridge; in the other, I held an empty 12-gauge casing. It was when I began playing on the table with the two units that I realized the possibility of a major breakthrough.

Suddenly, I told my father that I had an idea. I rushed out the door carrying only the empty casing. In the workshop, I used a hacksaw to saw off the brass portion of the shell close to the rim, creating an empty tube. Then I did a demonstration, showing Dad how neatly the 16-gauge shot shell slipped inside the empty 12-gauge tube. I explained that when this double assembly was loaded into the chamber, the smaller shell could no longer expand. Hence, there was a strong possibility that this might work.

Immediately we prepared for another test firing. When I pulled the trigger I knew by the sound of the blast and the intensity of the recoil that we were in business again. The shot-riddled can was struck with almost the same force as that produced by a 12-gauge, which is about all one could expect from a 16. I had successfully manufactured what may have been the world's only do-it-yourself 12-to-16-gauge modification kit.

With no longer any shortage of ammunition, we hunted the remainder of that winter, reaping the harvest made possible by our 12/16-gauge shotguns. Once again, necessity had become the mother of invention.

12

Water, Cockroaches, and Geologists

The problem began with a message from the office of the Superintendent of Lighthouses in Dartmouth. Apparently, someone in that office was responsible for the health and well-being of lightkeepers and their families. Suddenly, there was a concern about our water supply. The message stated the water in the cistern might be contaminated and not fit for human consumption.

The message went on to say that it was imperative to drain off the present water reserve, and then remove all debris remaining in the bottom of the concrete tank. Finally, we would have to scrub out the entire container using a special disinfectant. Eventually, rainwater dripping off the roof would refill the cistern.

It was a tall order, not the sort of thing one would undertake without some careful planning. The water in the cistern was our only safe water supply: most of the streams on the island contain tannin-stained water. The tannins reacting with air created strange-looking suds that settled in tiny pools as the water tumbled over the rocks. Dad decided that, while this operation was underway, we could haul our water from the old abandoned reservoir about half a mile down the road.

Shortly after receiving the orders from head office, Dad and I loaded two wooden barrels onto the wagon and hitched it to the tractor. We motored down the trail. Since there was no room to turn around at the reservoir, we continued on down to the landing. On the return trip we stopped at the reservoir and off-loaded the water barrels. Using a rubber hose, my father siphoned the water out of the reservoir and into the barrels. After they were filled, a wooden plug was inserted into the filler holes and the barrels were flipped over on their sides in preparation for reloading.

Much toil and strain could have been eliminated here, if either the reservoir were higher up the bank or the road elevation were lower. Then there would have been enough of an incline for the water to flow into the barrels while they were still on the wagon. The runoff from the reservoir had made the road in front if it soft and muddy. Using two planks for a ramp, we began rolling each barrel into the wagon. Our arms and backs were straining under the weight, while our feet, searching for traction, were slipping and sliding in the mud. Finally, with much difficulty, the barrels were rolled back into the wagon. Slowly we motored back to the station, being careful not to break the fragile wooden casks as the wagon bounced over the bumpy trail.

The barrels were unloaded and positioned horizontally on a makeshift stand, from which the water could easily be drained off. With our supply of fresh water in place, we were ready for the next step. A few feet from the house, at a point where the grade was equal to the bottom of the cistern, there was a large drain plug. It was overgrown with grass and had to be dislodged from the ground. This was the end of the cistern drain. When we opened the valve a torrent of muddy water gushed out. Here was the proof that there was dirt in our water, and we certainly hadn't realized how much. It didn't take long for this large drain pipe to completely empty the cistern.

Access to the cistern was through a hatch in the kitchen floor. This was one part of the house that I had never explored, and when my father dropped a ladder through the hole, I scrambled down to investigate. It was no surprise that it was dark and damp as I climbed down the ladder, but when I stepped on the cistern floor I was shocked to find that it was covered with about four inches of muck.

One could only guess as to how it got there, or how long it had taken to collect that much dirt. At that time there was little acid pollution to contaminate the rain, and it fell from the sky in its purest form. As the rainwater poured off the roof, it was captured by the eaves trough and funnelled into the cistern by downspouts on either side of the house. One would expect that a roof located far from the dust and pollution of any city would be relatively clean. The origin of this dirt would remain a mystery.

However, the remains of an earlier problem that we had encountered during our first year in the house may have contributed to some of the muck: the house was infested with cockroaches. Normally this kind of a problem would be associated with poor housekeeping. My mother was meticulously clean, but the bugs already in the house had no intention of leaving just because she came to live there. We had to live with an infestation of these loathesome insects for almost a year.

We were careful not to blame the previous tenants for inviting them, nor did we criticize them for not eradicating them. These insects were common aboard many ships of that day, and they probably came ashore as stowaways in the boxes of supplies delivered to the light station. Once they began to multiply, there seemed to be no way to stop them.

As soon as the cockroaches were discovered, we did our best to make them uncomfortable. My parents knew roaches don't thrive in a clean house. Armed with pails of water and boxes of Spic and Span cleaner, we began operation clean-up. Mom and Dad scrubbed down the walls and the ceilings while Ina and I cleaned the floor, concentrating on the tiny cracks from which these bugs seemed to emerge. Finally, we painted every single room in the house.

We were able to conclude very quickly that cockroaches may indeed prefer a house that is damp and dirty, but are also quite content to live in one that is dry and clean. These unwelcome guests continued to visit us every night, even after all the toiling and straining we did to eliminate them. They literally came out of the woodwork, lured into the open by the dim and flickering light of our oil lamps. They came by the hundreds, especially from behind the door casings between the kitchen and the living room. Every night, using fly swatters, we killed as many as we could but by the following evening there seemed to be even more. After a long and losing battle with these determined pests, we retired to our bedrooms upstairs, where for some unknown reason, there were no cockroaches.

Their lack of interest in the bedrooms was more than offset by their occupation of Mom's pantry and the things inside the cupboard and under the counter. Those who study these insects tell us that they are very intelligent bugs, and one has to admire their persistence. Somehow, while we slept, they managed to get inside the boxes of food, where they would spend the night dining on the contents. Since we were bigger than they, and not willing to share our meal with them at the table, we could easily separate the cockroaches from the crackers and corn flakes. The situation became a little more sticky when these rascals got into the molasses and the corn syrup.

Unable to defeat them, and not willing to join them, Dad sent another message to the Superintendent of Lighthouses, requesting assistance. When the next supply ship arrived, we received a small bottle of a liquid chemical marked "DDT," guaranteed to exterminate cockroaches.

With the confidence that the scales were finally tipped in our favour, we marched into battle with the heavy artillery. To be on the safe side, our parents sent Ina and I outside during the spraying operation. Mom and Dad, each armed with a spray gun, travelled throughout the house blasting all the rooms, as well as every nook and cranny frequented by roaches. They sprayed inside all the cupboards, peering in through each door opening to be sure that they had not missed any place. After about an hour of doing battle with the unseen enemy of the night, Mom began to feel dizzy and nauseated. Dad felt similarly ill. By holding on to each other, they managed to stagger out of the house before they collapsed. In the fresh air, their condition quickly stabilized. At this point, Dad decided to read the warning label.

My father read instructions only when all else failed. The label stated that the chemical was highly toxic and should be sprayed indoors for a only a few seconds. The process could be repeated periodically until the insects were eliminated. Somehow, my parents managed to survive while breathing the toxic fumes for almost an hour without adequate ventilation. They had almost become victims of "friendly fire," causing my mother to cringe at the thought of what might have happened if two children were left alone on the island with dead parents. As for the cockroaches, they were not so lucky: after that final assault not a single one was ever seen again.

Meanwhile, back in the cistern, standing in ankle-deep muck, my mother mentioned a sickening possibility as to the origin of the mud. Could some of this accumulation be cockroach remains from the past? Those lads probably spent their daylight hours lounging around this big pool beneath the floor, the damp and dark environment a natural paradise for loathesome insects. Over the years how many would have fallen off the boards and the beams, their bodies slowly decomposing and piling up on the cistern floor? Whatever became of those that were sprayed with the poison? Did they all run in panic to take one final swim in the pool? At first, we thought that the idea to drain off all our water was a bit ridiculous, but maybe the people at the head office in Dartmouth had good reason to be concerned about our health.

With buckets, ropes, and shovels, the clean-up of the cistern got underway. I positioned myself firmly in the mud on the cistern floor while Dad lowered the first bucket for me to fill. After I had scooped it full of mud, he hoisted it up through the hatchway in the kitchen floor and carried it outside, where he disposed of it. This procedure continued for hours. When Mom found time to assist, she lowered a second bucket through the hole and a kind of bucket brigade got underway. When I could no longer shovel up any more mud, Mom and Dad came down with their mops and brooms and finished the final cleaning with the prescribed disinfectant. After several days of continuous work on the cistern, we finally closed the hatch in the floor and waited for the rain.

We had predicted it from the very beginning. Even though we waited patiently for the rain, we never really expected it. By draining off our water supply, we had left ourselves in a position to receive the full impact of Murphy's Law. Now, thanks to Mr. Murphy, we could expect plenty of sunshine with no chance of rain. In the meantime, we continued to haul our water from the reservoir. It was inconvenient, having to always step outside to get water from a barrel. Often I would forget and attempt to operate the hand pump, now sitting useless on the end of the cupboard. With great expectations I would plunge down the handle; the pump responded with only a dry snort. After a week or so, I could see my mother was becoming very annoyed with the water situation.

Once again Dad had an idea. We headed back to the reservoir. His plan was to haul water all day, in an effort to fill the cistern. By evening we had completed about a half dozen trips and poured twice as many barrels of water through the hole in the floor. With aching backs and sore muscles we dropped a ladder through the hatch, climbed down, and viewed the results. For all our labour we were rewarded with less than two inches of water on the cistern floor. It would take another six inches just to reach the foot valve on the hand pump. We decided to wait for the rain.

The water situation at the reservoir had also begun to deteriorate. The tiny stream of water that fed it had slowed to a trickle, and with little or no overflow, it was in danger of becoming stagnant. We could soon find ourselves here on this island in a situation not unlike that of the Ancient Mariner in Samuel Taylor Coleridge's poem, with "water, water everywhere . . . nor any drop to drink."

It was about this time that an unexpected visit from a fishing boat brought us the mail. It also dropped off some unusual human cargo. Four men, each wearing a backpack and carrying an odd-looking pick hammer, scrambled up the cliff. Three of them introduced themselves as student geologists from a university in New York state. They had come to St. Paul Island to obtain rock samples as part of their studies. The fourth man, tall, muscular, and older than the others, referred to himself as the "slave" because he would backpack the heavy samples to their base camp at Atlantic Cove. Although I do not remember their names, I do recall that they were a very friendly group and they all displayed a great sense of humour.

They intended to remain on the island for two weeks, making camp in one of the abandoned wireless residences. With the use of the tractor, we helped them move all their equipment and provisions up the hill. While they set up housekeeping inside, Dad chatted with them and answered most of their questions. He told them that water could be found at the reservoir just up the trail, but made no mention of our own water problems. They appeared to have everything that they required, yet Dad was quick to offer our assistance if they had a problem. As we were leaving, Mom, in her usual style, promised that she would have them up to our house some evening for dinner.

The following day, I saw the students and their technician out on the cliffs just beyond the winch building. They were busy chipping off small rock particles and carefully examining each piece with a special magnifying lens. Each sample was tagged and placed inside the backpack for transportation back to camp. I stood there for some time watching them with intense curiosity, hoping at any moment they might discover some valuable mineral. If that happened, I expected them to drop their picks and begin dancing on the rocks, like an old prospector in some western movie. Actually, these men were more interested in studying the rock's formation in the earth's crust than in searching for mineral deposits. I finally grew tired of watching them when their work seemed to lack excitement.

During their stay we would often see them perched high upon a rocky ledge, or down in some deep crevice, the sea sweeping in and churning around them. On a couple of occasions we observed them working in areas that we had always considered inaccessible, or at least unsafe to negotiate on foot. We assumed that they were skilled climbers who were trained to navigate safely over such hostile terrain.

One day while hiking back to Atlantic Cove, they became exhausted and were very glad to see us come along in our boat. When we found them, they were having little success in their effort to scale a steep, smooth cliff in order to reach the safety of the trees and the trail above. They had been trapped on this small point for several hours. They joyfully accepted our helping hand and we gave them a relaxing cruise back to the landing.

One evening while they were at our house for dinner, one of the geologists shared a story with us about a narrow escape a few days earlier. They had just completed taking samples from the rocks on Norwegian Head when he noticed a bald eagle's nest in a stunted spruce tree high above him. No doubt the eagle had wisely selected this location to raise her family, safely situated on a steep slope at the edge of a nearly vertical cliff. This curious geologist, tempted by the challenge, took it upon himself to scale the cliff, climb the tree and look into the nest. He must have been motivated by the same reasoning used by Sir Edmund Hillary when he climbed Mt. Everest – because it was there. While the others watched, he carefully manoeuvred himself across the face of the cliff and eventually reached the tree.

He did not expect the welcome he received as he reached the top of the tree and the nest. You could call it bad timing, for it was at that moment that the female eagle returned and found the intruder at her door. She swooped down, her fearsome beak aimed to strike the unwelcome guest, while her powerful claws were set to hang on for the kill. Being in no position to defend himself from a large, angry bird, the geologist beat a hasty but somewhat careless retreat. Our man lost his balance when a limb suddenly snapped, sending him tumbling to the ground. Had he not quickly grabbed a tree root he would have certainly continued the descent to the bottom of the cliff. There was some discussion among the men as to whether or not he would have survived the fall. He may have fallen into the ocean far below and perhaps survived, or his body could have struck a ledge of rock at the base of the cliff and St. Paul would have claimed another victim. Fortunately this time the island was content to teach this man a lesson about the respect it demands from all who come to visit.

The geology crew came to our house for dinner a couple more times, and Mom would usually send a care package for them each time we went to the landing. They especially enjoyed Mom's freshly baked bread with a bottle of her cranberry jam. Another time Dad and I gave them a large cod fish that we jigged just off the cove. When their departure date was delayed because of rough seas around the island, their food became increasingly scarce. Once again we sent them a box of canned goods as well as anything else we could spare, and they were more than grateful to receive these packages.

Meanwhile, we were still struggling with our water problems, and when it appeared that everything had already gone wrong that could go wrong we were surprised to find the Murphy's Law guy was working a little overtime. In what had now become our routine, each evening Dad and I loaded our two empty water barrels aboard the wagon and headed out for our rendezvous with the reservoir. One evening as we were rounding the last curve on the trail before the dam, I was puzzled by the appearance of a strange white foam visible through the trees. The puzzlement turned to shock when we saw the pillows of soapsuds being generated by four naked geologists bathing in our reservoir. We didn't even stop – just kept on going with our water barrels as though we had some other destination in mind. It seemed like the only thing to do, in order to avoid embarrassment to them or us. We could not blame them because Dad had never informed them about our water shortage and the importance of the reservoir.

Since the water was still barely flowing, the suds lasted for several days, forcing us to move upstream for drinking water. It seemed to take forever to fill even a small jug with such a tiny trickle of water, but we persevered. For a while it looked as though we might have to hike into one of the lakes, but it was rumoured that its water was unfit to drink. A few days after our guests left the island, the rains finally came and re-plenished our cistern.

The morning our visitors left the island we were there at the land-ing to see them off. The rock samples had been transferred to wooden boxes and one of the men was busy nailing down the covers when we arrived. Each box was carefully placed aboard the small dory before be-ing rowed out to the fishing boat anchored in the cove. After the last box was stowed aboard, all the men left together. There were the usual goodbyes as we all stood upon the bank. Although I never remembered their names, I would never forget that group. They were interesting as well as entertaining, and their brief visit to our island enabled us to share a small portion of our lives with them. The small boat pulled away from the cove, and silence once again settled over the station.

When the Christmas supply ship came the following December, Mom received what she regarded as the greatest gift of all. It came in a plain ordinary envelope but when she read the enclosed letter, the joy she felt inside blossomed over her face and a tear rolled down her cheek. It was a well-written and fairly lengthy thank-you note from the mother of one of the student geologists. In the letter, the lady expressed her deepest appreciation for all that we had done for her son and his friends while they were with us on St. Paul Island. A special thanks was extend-ed to my mother for all the dinners she had prepared and other food items she had sent down to their camp. The woman admitted that the boys probably came to the island somewhat unprepared for the mission and their success was due in part to my mother's hospitality. Mom never forgot that letter and even today she still cherishes it in her heart.

13

A Winter of Sickness

Sickness: it was my mother's greatest fear and the main reason she was apprehensive about going to St. Paul Island in the first place. Upon her arrival, she found nothing that would alleviate her concerns. The distant silhouette of Cape Breton, visible only on clear days, gave her little comfort. If anyone in our family should require medical attention, the nearest facility was located at Neil's Harbour, nearly twenty-six miles away. She had reason to be concerned: those twenty-six miles spanned one of the wildest stretches of the North Atlantic, virtually impassable in winter due to drift ice. There was indeed a certain amount of risk involved living in such isolation. I never gave it much thought, and we all took life one day at a time. The radio telephone, our only means of communication, was tested daily and always available should we need to call for help.

Deciding to send a message for help was a serious matter. It could be difficult to know when the sickness was serious enough to justify making an emergency call. Upon receiving a call for assistance, the federal Department of Transportation would dispatch one of their supply ships to rescue the sick individual. If there were no ships in the area, or if a lifeboat could not land safely, a Navy helicopter would be called upon to carry out the mission. The choppers were based in Halifax, more than 250 miles away. My father wanted to avoid the embarrassment of causing an unnecessary and very expensive rescue operation in a situation where the person would have recovered without medical attention.

My father made an excellent example of himself when he awoke one morning with a stomach ache. His first reaction was to seek help from a wooden chest of simple medicine (provided by the government for minor injuries and illnesses). It contained little more than what might be found in an average bathroom medicine cabinet. There were some bandages, iodine, and several large brown bottles of patent medicines. We found Frier's Balsam (swallowed with a little sugar) excellent for a cough, although the instructions on the bottle warned against it being taken internally. Some of the medicines could be taken internally, pending the approval of a medical doctor. With one year of high school education, my father was the nearest we had to a doctor. After careful consultation with my mother, he chose a medicine, swallowed a little and waited for the results.

When he awoke the following morning, the pain in his stomach had intensified. He managed to attend to his duties at the lighthouse and to help my mother with some household chores, but we did no duck hunting or any other outdoor activity. His condition worsened over the next few days. Finally, he was getting out of bed only to attend to the lighthouse. Mom anxiously urged him to request an air rescue, but Dad insisted that he would be okay. He put off making that call, always waiting until the next scheduled radio telephone check, hoping for an improvement in his condition.

After about a week of suffering, Dad realized he would have to leave us to get medical help. Before he left he wanted to make certain we could operate the light in his absence. In order to prove we were capable, he tested my mother and me. He had us light the light ourselves on a couple of occasions. The only part of the operation with which I had any difficulty was pumping up the air tank to the required pressure. But with a great deal effort and determination (as well as a little help from Mom) the gauge on the tank finally read forty pounds.

Convinced now that we could keep the light, he promised to send a message for help the next day on the morning radio schedule. When he awoke the following day, however, it wasn't necessary to make that call. Sometime during the night his pain had left him as quickly as it had come. This time, the waiting game had paid off. But to expect time to always be the cure could be a serious mistake, especially in winter.

Ofttimes during the winter months a heavy glaze of ice covered the ground surrounding the entire station. It made walking not just difficult but extremely dangerous. Our whole yard was a steep grade; we had only the fence to separate us from the cliff and Eternity. We had learned with the sleigh that the fence was not always reliable as a guardrail. If we wanted to walk safely anywhere on the property, something had to done.

As usual, Dad had a solution. Actually it was something he had seen done before. He cut out several strips of sheet metal and bent each piece around the soles of each of our boots. Once each unit was shaped for the boots, he removed it and used a nail to punch holes down through the base of each tin piece. The jagged edges of the exit holes provided traction on the ice. After he attached straps to these metal grips, we secured them to our boots and safely walked on the icy surfaces around the station.

The ice grips were rather cumbersome, and it was time-consuming to lash them to our boots every time we left the house. One day Ina chose to leave the house without them and risk making the few steps to the workshop. Ina's boots had worn out prematurely that year, and she wore wool socks over them to hold the flapping soles and sides together. Only a few minutes after she left the house, she returned screaming and crying. Blood was pouring from her mouth when she entered the door, and Mom, in a state of panic, tried in vain to comfort her.

Sitting Ina in a chair, Mom checked the injury and heard the details about the accident. Ina had slipped on the ice, hitting her head when she fell. There was no injury to the back of her head, but the sudden jolt caused a tooth to deeply pierce her tongue. Mom and Dad both worked on Ina, holding pressure against the wound with pieces of gauze in an effort to reduce the bleeding. This injury would need the attention of a doctor or at least some medical advice.

That evening, my father sent a message that was relayed to a doctor in Sydney. He gave the details of the injury, and asked if it were possible to administer an effective treatment there on the island. Next morning, we received the typical ambiguous reply one generally receives from a doctor. He said, "If the wound was a cut, it would require stitches and she would have to be transported to a medical facility. However, if the injury was a hole, it would eventually heal on its own." Also, he warned, it was important to watch out for infection.

For the remainder of that week, Mom and Dad spent much of their time arguing about whether or not Ina had a hole or a cut in her tongue. While they were debating the situation, her tongue was slowly healing on its own. Dad would have Ina stick out her tongue for inspection several times a day, since infection was now the main concern. I was sure this daily exercise would cause her tongue to extend out so far she'd be able to lick her forehead by the time the tongue healed.

In the early part of January, 1957, my mother began complaining about a sore throat. Like most mothers, she spent much of her time worrying about the consequences of others becoming ill, but gave little thought to her own health. Now, fate forced her to take interest in her own well-being.

The days passed, but I could see there was no improvement in Mom's condition. She was having difficulty swallowing, and quite often I observed her holding her throat as if trying to ease the pain. Dad thought that perhaps a small particle of food, such as a bone, had lodged in her throat. Over the next few days, my father suggested various theories for her discomfort. Mom was not convinced, and was saying nothing.

Mom, being more of a pessimist, diagnosed her condition as far more grave than anything Dad had suggested or could even imagine. Unknown to me, but still fresh in my mother's memory, was a minor operation she had several years before. It was a very simple operation, but the surgery had been performed to remove what the doctor referred to as a "cancerous growth" on her lip. Now, she was almost certain that the cancer had spread to her throat.

Worry causes things to become worse. My mother excelled at worrying, and her condition deteriorated correspondingly. Often I would see her sitting crying, but she still managed to prepare the meals and do most of her housework. After seeing my mother in misery for nearly ten days with no sign of improvement, Dad determined it was time to send a message for help.

It was shortly after the regular morning radio check that Dad began calling: "VCO North Sydney radio, this is Southwest St. Paul, we have an emergency. Do you copy?"

He repeated this message over and over for hours, with no reply. Finally, just before the regular evening radio check, Dad got a response. Through a relayed message, he described his wife's condition to a physician. The doctor strongly urged that she be transported to a hospital immediately. Since this was an emergency situation, the radio operator ask my father to "stand by" for further information. Dad suspected that the *Edward Cornwallis* would probably be dispatched to the scene; he had seen the ship in the area only a few days before. About an hour later a radio message confirmed Dad's theory: the *Edward Cornwallis* would arrive around noon the following day.

The road to the landing was the only problem now. Several recent snowstorms had struck the island, leaving more than two feet of snow on parts of the trail. The road was impassable by tractor, and Mom was in no condition to walk.

Perhaps it was just luck, or maybe it was a classic example of the truth behind the statement, "When God closes a door, He opens a window." Seldom was the water calm on the Southwest Point of St. Paul Island in winter. Looking down from the lighthouse that day, Dad could scarcely see a ripple on the water or any surf on the shore. Next day, when the *Edward Cornwallis* arrived, the sea was still unusually calm. Dad made arrangements with the captain to send the lifeboat into Jessie Cove (named after the ill-fated ship) located on the western side of the point near the lighthouse. Mom would need to walk only about three hundred yards to board the launch.

We were grateful for the short hike, but for Mom it was not an easy one. Even though it was downhill for the most part, she struggled, her shorter leg dragging in the deep snow. Dad helped her along, but still her steps were short, awkward and uneven. The hem of her coat trailed behind, sweeping a pattern in the snow delineating her unsteady gait.

The last two hundred feet would be difficult for anyone to walk. The trail cut across a steep slope along the top of high cliffs. I found that particular section breathtaking to cross on bare ground. It was mainly loose gravel, devoid of any vegetation. With no solid footing nor anything to hold, one slip here would result in a short slide and a ninety-foot drop into the ocean. On this occasion, the situation was much worse: this area was covered with nearly a foot of hard packed snow. My father came to our rescue. He tested the firmness of the snow, and then stomped a trail of foot holes across the slope. We followed carefully, making sure that each step was planted firmly into the rut. I dragged my mother's suitcase and tried to hold back my tears. Ina was behind me; I noticed that she was already crying openly. Finally we arrived on the cliff overlooking Jessie Cove. Just off the beach below, the ship's launch was standing by.

Descending the cliff was the easy part. One of the previous lightkeepers, perhaps anticipating just such an emergency, had spent a great deal of time and effort building a crude set of wooden steps down the granite face. This ladder-like assembly was constructed mainly from pieces of driftwood, resembling something out of *Robinson Crusoe*. Dad and I had built a handrail for added safety. We con-

My mother, Ina and me on the steps at Jessie Cove.

tinually replaced rotten rungs, using any suitable driftwood that washed up on the beach.

Mom slowly made her way down the ladder, then gingerly walked to the water's edge where the launch was waiting. It was a sombre scene when Mom turned to kiss us all goodbye. She gathered Ina and I into her arms, giving us a desperate hug. After one last look at her family, she stepped aboard the small boat. One of the crew took her by the arm and escorted her to a thwart. As another man started the motor, Mom called out plaintively, "Goodbye, Freddy!"

The remaining three of us walked back to the station and sat on the concrete base of the lighthouse. From there we watched as the launch was hoisted aboard the ship. We remained at our post until the *Edward Cornwallis* became a small speck in the distance. It was bound for the city of Sydney, sixty miles away, well beyond our horizon. Reluctantly, we returned to the house where, that night, no one would be waiting for us.

Dad now had to become Mr. Mom. He prepared the meals, did the laundry, and looked after Ina and me, in much the same manner as Mom. I noticed, however, that his method of scrubbing the floor was different from my mother's. She got down on her hands and knees with a scrub brush, whereas Dad, standing up, used only a mop and a pail of water. He said, "My way is better and a whole lot faster."

Mom's absence brought a few changes to our lifestyle. There would be no more duck hunting: we couldn't take Ina with us, and we couldn't leave her at home. I was already well ahead of schedule in my schoolwork, but I used this extra time to cover even more lessons. This turned out to be a wise move and paid off before the school year came to an end.

A few days after Mom left us, we received a radio message from the doctor with his diagnosis of her condition. She was suffering from a severe throat infection which was being treated with antibiotics. We were relieved to hear that her ailment was not serious, and this message greatly lifted our spirits. She was released from the hospital seven days after she left the island.

Returning to the island proved to be far more difficult than leaving it. While waiting for transportation to be arranged, Mom stayed with one of her relatives in North Sydney. She came to the radio station several times a week in order to talk to us. It was good to hear her voice again. The radio operator kindly permitted the conversation to continue for a considerable length of time.

Each time she spoke with us, she expressed more frustration about the continuing delays by the government officials arranging her transportation. Every week, they told her that one of their ships would pick her up next week, but, when next week came, she was informed that the ship was stuck in the ice somewhere. One week the promise was broken when the ship was used to free a sealing vessel caught in the ice; the next time, the ship was diverted to a fishing boat needing assistance. As the weeks passed it became apparent that the stranded wife of a lighthouse keeper did not rate very high on the government's list of priorities.

Nearly five weeks after she left the island, on February 20th, we received word that Mom was on her way, and she was coming first class. We never learned whether it was compassion or if the government officials simply tired of listening to her complain, but something prompted them to dispatch a helicopter to fly her back home.

At the news of her impending arrival, Ina, Dad and I gathered outside. We sat on a rock, to watch and listen. I heard the beating of rotors first, then Dad saw the helicopter. First it was just a dot on the horizon, flying low over the drift ice. Then, in a few minutes, it was hovering over our roof. Gazing skyward, listening to the deafening noise, I could see my mother looking through the window.

It was tricky to land with no level terrain on which to set the chopper down. The pilot rested one wheel on the sod while he kept the aircraft level using the thrust of the spinning rotor. The co-pilot helped my mother exit the aircraft and stay low in order to avoid the deadly spinning rotors. After being without a mother for such a long time, we were jubilant to be together again. The jubilation would be short-lived: before that season ended, another illness would cause us to repeat the experience.

It came on very slowly at first. Just a small ache in my abdomen, not enough discomfort to even mention to my parents. When it became more annoying and started to last longer, I told my mother about it. Mom and Dad discussed all the possibilities, and their diagnosis changed from day to day. They made me try various medicines from that familiar box, but nothing relieved the knot in my stomach.

It could never be described as pain, but the feeling made it uncomfortable for me to be involved with outdoor play or activity. When I lost interest in hunting, Mom knew the situation was serious. I became frustrated doing schoolwork, and suggested that perhaps it was the long hours I spent bent over my desk that was causing the discomfort in my stomach. My erector set, which until now had given me many hours of enjoyment, sat idle on its table in a corner of the living room. I complained constantly and my parents were becoming very concerned about my health.

One morning, Mom noticed that I was having difficulty with the simple task of getting dressed. She also saw me behaving oddly, apparently disoriented and forgetful. I was unable to do simple things that should have required no thought at all. When she asked me about it, I could not explain it. I heard Dad say that he had often seen me sitting and staring at the wall with unseeing eyes for long periods of time. They both became increasingly worried and agreed I might be suffering from some kind of brain disease.

This revelation came to them one morning just after the regular radio schedule. This should not have been a problem, because the operators at VCO Marine Radio Station were supposed to monitor our frequency at all times. Dad began calling on the radio telephone, "VCO North Sydney Radio, this is Southwest St. Paul, we have an emergency."

But there was no reply. He repeated the call time and time again but heard only the monotonous sound of static. Then he added a little more to the text of the transmission saying, "Anyone hearing this distress call, please contact VCO North Sydney Marine Radio."

This would be an excellent, and yet a terrible, time for my grandfather to be listening on his shortwave radio. Grandfather, in his home at Neil's Harbour, had a marine band receiver which he used to monitor all our schedules. He liked hearing my father's voice, thus reassuring himself that we were all okay. If he was listening, and the shock from the text of the transmission did not kill him, he would call for help. However, since this was between schedules, it was unlikely Grandpa would have his receiver turned on.

Fortunately, someone else was listening. On board a distant Coast Guard icebreaker, a radio operator scanning the frequencies heard my father's frantic SOS call. He immediately contacted VCO on another frequency and forwarded the information.

It was almost noon when the radio finally crackled to life, with the voice of the North Sydney radio operator calling Southwest St. Paul. Dad quickly informed him that his son was very ill and required immediate medical attention. He was asked to "stand by." Almost an hour later, the operator informed us that a Navy helicopter would be leaving Halifax shortly for St. Paul Island. Weather permitting, their expected time of arrival would be about 6 p.m. AST.

Plans were made and suitcases were packed once again. Mom and Ina would accompany me, leaving my father alone on the island. This time when the helicopter arrived, just before dark, there was little excitement. The co-pilot ushered the three of us aboard. Through the window of the chopper's noisy cabin, I could see my father standing there alone in the twilight. Then we were jerked into the air, swept out over the ice, and bound for Sydney.

At Sydney Airport, a car was waiting to transport us to St. Elizabeth's Hospital in North Sydney. I was admitted immediately upon arrival. When Mom and Ina left my room, I tried to sleep. But I couldn't, because I thought I was going to die – die before I had a chance to figure out why I was born in the first place. There were all those things I had thought so much about on St. Paul . . . now I would have to leave them unresolved forever.

Even though our days on the island were filled with school activities, duck hunting and various forms of entertainment, there was still time to think – in fact, too much time. At that time, the space program was just getting underway. The news often told about the difficulties the spacecraft were having breaking free of the earth's gravity. This new science caused me to think about the subject of gravity, and I spent hours trying to determine what caused it. I thought I had it figured out once. I knew that the earth constantly travelled through space, so therefore, when I leaped from an object I did not really go down; instead the earth came up to meet me. However, I took a closer look at the globe and saw that if folks on the other side, in Australia for instance, did the same experiment, they should keep on going up. It was back to the drawing board.

One question always led to another. For instance, if we were constantly moving through space (as the text books said) when would we reach the end of space? The sky must end somewhere. Furthermore, on our journey through space we would surely meet God somewhere along the way. I wondered why He needed me, and how I was intended to fit into the universal picture. Slowly, I had become obsessed with the mysteries of the universe and the meaning of life. I wasn't aware that constantly thinking about such things can be hazardous to your health.

I awoke the next morning in my hospital bed with two nurses leaning over me. One of those troublesome subjects must have been still fresh on my mind for when I saw these ladies in white I knew they had all the answers.

"I need to know," I said, "where does the sky end?"

Somewhat stunned, they looked at each other with corrugated brows. Then they looked at me. It was as though I had come from some distant galaxy on the outer fringes of the universe.

Later that morning the doctor came to see me. After he made a brief examination, I began to discuss with him some of those perplexing and unsolved mysteries which I had wrestled with for so long. If he had any answers, he was not about to share them with me. He just sat there and listened to my rambling. He stayed only long enough to diagnose my condition and later he informed my mother that I was suffering from severe emotional anxiety. He explained that it was something that is seldom seen in a nine-year-old child, but treatment was available. I was released from the hospital about a week later, with several months' supply of little white "anti-think" pills. The mysterious illness was gone, and with it went my deep mysterious thoughts.

While waiting for transportation back to the island, the three of us stayed at the home of my Great-Aunt Melissa and Great-Uncle Enoch, which for me was quite an experience. It took me quite some time to become familiar with their lifestyle. They were devout members of the Seventh Day Adventist faith. Out of respect for our hosts, Mom made us go to their church on Saturday, and then, on Sunday morning, we would go to our Presbyterian church. It seemed as though we were spending the entire weekend in church.

Though their religion did not approve of eating certain food, Aunt Melissa was still a good cook. When she called us to the table, I approached it with mixed emotions, in spite of the fact that I was hungry and the meal smelled delicious. The problem was the blessing of the food.

Giving thanks to God for our food was not new to me. At our table on St. Paul Island we always said the blessing – just a few short words before we ate. At Uncle Enoch's home it was much different. We had to kneel down on the floor with our heads bowed and elbows on our chairs. Then Uncle Enoch would begin to pray. The blessing would last for twenty minutes or more, during which Uncle Enoch would mention a long list of subjects that included the names of sick people, various places in trouble around the world, and other disturbing events in the news. Finally, his prayer ended with something about a new heaven and a new earth. Often I wondered if it were possible to starve to death with so much food above my head.

There was one time Uncle Enoch probably thought that I had died and gone to that new heaven. The kitchen was warm that day, and I was kneeling at my chair beside the hot wood stove. My head was bowed and I could feel myself becoming quite dizzy. Uncle Enoch prayed on, his voice fading off into the distance. Suddenly, I fainted and collapsed on my face across the floor. I awoke a short time later in my mother's arms. I never knew if my uncle stopped the long blessing after I passed out or whether he continued on to the end.

Almost every day, their grandson, Douglas, came over to visit. He and I would sit on the porch and talk. We had a lot to share, as he too had been ill and hospitalized for some time. Douglas was a very intelligent boy, who seemed to have a vast knowledge of almost every subject, especially things pertaining to hospitals and doctors. He was just the sort of person with whom I could have entered into a discussion about those deep thoughts that had troubled me for so long. I never mentioned them though. I suspect those "anti-think pills" the doctor prescribed for me were kicking in. Usually when he came to visit he would bring along a pack of cards or a bag of marbles and we would play for hours on the back step. This helped to pass the time, as the days went by slowly waiting for transportation back to St. Paul Island.

Aunt Melissa was a kind and gentle person, but I always found her conversations with my mother to be very depressing. I overheard her speak at length about some of her friends and relatives who were sick and dying. She was very descriptive and she included all of the disturbing details. What particularly troubled me was that for the most part, she talked about her grandson, Douglas. He had recently been released from a Halifax hospital where he had undergone surgery for a brain tumour. I could sense that she was very upset, and based on her conversation it seemed that my new friend Douglas was not expected to live very long.

Almost every evening Mom, Ina and I would walk over to the marine radio station at the top of Marconi Hill on the other side of town. There we spoke with Dad, and as I listened nightly to his conversation, one could detect an air of sadness in his voice. During our absence it was not total solitude for Dad; by this time the drift ice had disappeared, and he had visited aboard a couple of fishing boats that had stopped by the island.

When it was my turn at the microphone I would often tell him about some amusing thing that had happened to me recently. It must not have been very funny, or he was not in a mood for laughing. Mom, as usual, talked in great detail about all the disappointments and delays experienced in trying to arrange government transportation. Her tales of woe were similar to those I had heard so often, about three months before. Each time she ended her transmission with the words, "We're all looking forward to seeing you in a few days," but it was not to be.

On the morning of May 16th, nearly four weeks after I was released from the hospital, we received word that we were going home. The *Edward Cornwallis* was docked at the pier in North Sydney and would depart for St. Paul Island early the next morning. They wanted us on board that night. Homesick and uncomfortable where we were living, I longed to go aboard immediately and not wait until evening. Of course we could not because of various commitments, as well as all those goodbyes. I raced down the street to tell Douglas about the good news and to say goodbye to him and his sisters. Without him, the time spent in North Sydney would have been almost unbearable.

Over the years I would see Douglas several times. His tumour went into remission and remained so for nearly eighteen years. Perhaps it was due, in whole or in part, to his grandfather's faith, lifting up Douglas's name so many times in those long mealtime prayers. But sadly, in April of 1974, Douglas passed away.

On the evening of our departure from North Sydney, we took a taxi to the pier and boarded the *Edward Cornwallis*. When I awoke the next morning, we were well on our way to the island. It would have been much better for me had I remained asleep. The ship was tossing and turning with such intensity that I could scarcely stay in my berth. Mom and Ina were already up. They were both extremely seasick, and within a few minutes I joined them at the bucket in the cabin. At about that time the ship's cook came into our cabin and asked if we would like something to eat. No one answered him; the green colour of our faces was probably the only answer he needed.

With difficulty, I staggered over to the porthole and took a look outside. I saw watery valleys roll up and transform into mountainous seas, while the wind blew off their fleecy tops in a shower of spray. We had a wild ride for a while, then suddenly everything became calm. When I stepped out on the deck we were anchored in the peaceful waters off St. Paul's windward shore. We were home at last.

It was a happy reunion with Dad that day at the landing, especially after he told me about a puppy that I would be getting some day soon. My very own dog, he thought, would better occupy my time. Thus ended a long and hard winter of sickness. The rest of our days spent on St. Paul Island were without sickness, except for one small incident that happened a few years later.

It could not have happened at a better time; it could not have happened at a worse time. It was mid-September, and the *Lady Laurier* was preparing to deliver the annual supplies to St. Paul Island. On the day the ship began unloading the annual supplies for the Northeast light station, I began to develop a toothache.

This should not have happened. Each year during the vacation period we made several trips to the dentist to ensure that we had no cavities, or any other problems that might later cause pain. Dad wanted to avoid the ordeal involved in having one of us removed from the island for such a simple, and yet painful, illness as a toothache.

There are times when it seems that you just cannot win and nature will have the final say. Dad kept hoping that my toothache would pass, but as the day progressed the pain intensified. Throughout the night it throbbed continuously, and Mom stayed with me at my bedside. Nothing in that wonderful medicine chest would relieve the pain. The following morning Dad realized he would have to contact the captain of the *Lady Laurier*. He would ask him to take my mother and me into Dingwall, the nearest village on the mainland, in order to have a tooth extraction done at the doctor's office in Neil's Harbour

The chance of my illness occurring during those few days of the year when a ship was at the island was very remote. Yet my father was very reluctant to seize the opportunity. In fact, it was probably the most difficult call he would ever have to make in his entire career. It seemed a common coincidence back then, amongst various island lighthouse keepers along the coast, that people only became ill when there was a government ship in their area. This resulted in that ship having to leave its normal duties and transport a lighthouse keeper's wife, child or an assistant to a distant town in order to visit a doctor. This would infuriate my father and I would often hear him say, "That woman is not sick; she just wants to go ashore to visit her mother!" Or, "I know that man they're taking ashore now, and he only wants to get to a liquor store." No doubt there was some truth in what he was thinking, but the captain was obliged to do his duty and assume the individual was really ill.

Dad finally did make the call. The captain agreed to pick us up that afternoon, as soon as they completed unloading at the Northeast. I know that my father felt that the captain was probably thinking something like, "Now, you too, huh!"

When the launch came ashore that afternoon, it was the dirtiest boat I had ever seen. It was not fitting for any lady to step aboard. Small lumps of coal covered the entire bottom of the boat. There was coal on the thwarts and on the gunwales. Every supporting surface in the boat was covered with black dust. It appeared that the crew did not have time to clean out the launch, and came for us as soon as the last shovelful of coal had been removed. I was in too much pain to be concerned about a messy boat.

When we stepped aboard it was not the coal dust that made me reluctant to sit – quite the contrary. Some thoughtful crewman had taken the time to prepare a place for us to sit by spreading a clean light-coloured sheet across the rear thwart. A portion of this sheet was draped over the lumps of coal in the bottom of the boat. This clean sheet seemed so out of place that I felt a little ashamed to even sit on it.

If the captain was watching me come aboard his ship, he should have known that I was in genuine pain just by the look on my face. I wasn't that good an actor. I'm sure that everyone on board knew that this was no phony mission of mercy.

It was after dark when we arrived off Dingwall. The harbour is very shallow, and we went ashore by lifeboat. Across the road from the dock was a small convenience store, the Highland Heart Canteen. Mom knew the man who owned it. She hired him to take us to Neil's Harbour, about a twenty minute drive. The doctor was waiting for us, and in no time at all the tooth was extracted.

On the way back, we made a brief stopover at the home of my grandparents, which was not far from the doctor's office. When we stepped into the kitchen, Grandpa was reading a letter. He lifted up his eyes, and I saw his colour change as though he had just seen a ghost. We had caught him by surprise. Because this trip had been arranged between regular radio schedules, he had missed the news about our unexpected visit. The letter he was reading was from my mother.

After a brief conversation and enough hugs to last for nine more months, we were on our way again. As we drove off, it was sad to see my grandparents standing in the kitchen doorway alone. We lived so close to them, and yet so very far away.

We spent the night on board the *Lady Laurier* and, as usual, left for the island early the next morning. I spent most of the return voyage holding a cloth against my sore gums and rinsing out my mouth with salted water.

My aching jaw caused me to miss out on a once-in-a-lifetime opportunity. In my cabin I could hear the familiar throb of the steam engine and feel its power pushing us through the water. I had heard that this ship was soon to be scrapped; she was the last steam-driven Canadian government supply ship. This was my last chance to see a steam engine in motion, but Mom didn't want to ask for a guided tour nor did I feel well enough to visit the engine room. I have always regretted having missed such a unique experience.

It was still quite early in the morning when we arrived back at the island. As we motored ashore, I stole one final look at the *Lady Laurier* as she rode at anchor. She sailed away from the island later that day and never returned. The black smoke pouring from the stack waved her final farewell.

14

Ice, Seals, and More Ice

The picture on the calendar seemed inappropriate for the month of March. The scene depicted a lazy stream flowing through a green meadow. A boy wearing a short-sleeved shirt and rolled-up trousers was sitting on the bank with a fishing pole in his hand. He was enjoying the warmth of the spring sunshine while waiting for a fish to bite his hook. This scene did little to warm me one cold morning, as I watched my father re-light the fire in the kitchen stove. A partial cup of leftover coffee sat frozen on the table.

The world viewed through our kitchen window bore no resemblance to that picture on the calendar. Even though spring would officially begin in a few weeks, there was nothing outside to indicate a warming trend. Temperatures were still dipping to 0°F. Quite often the water in the short length of pipe on our hand pump would freeze just beneath the floor. Whenever that occurred, my father would have to use a blowtorch to heat the pipe to melt the ice.

Although March spelled the beginning of spring on the calendar, it was still the dead of winter on St. Paul Island. Gales of wind that paused only long enough to catch their breath or change directions continued to blast us, and were usually accompanied by snow. The glaze of ice covering the ground had increased dramatically in thickness. Between our house and the garage, the ice was well over a foot thick. Like a miniature glacier, it had slowly rolled down the hillside, slid through the fence and spilled out over the cliff. If it were not for the fence and the grips we installed on our boots, it would be extremely dangerous to walk anywhere outside our house. However, the pathway leading to the lighthouse was virtually ice free, because of the rocky terrain and the absence of a flow of water.

Our ice problem originated in a swamp located just a few paces up the hill from our house. Here, water constantly oozed up out of the ground, forming a small pond. In the summer, the overflow from the pond tumbled over the rocks, made its way through a shallow drain, over the cliff and into the sea. In the winter, the trickling water in the tiny creek froze solid. After that, the water from the swamp was influenced more by the wind. Throughout the winter the changing direction of the wind spread the water around the station, creating a virtual rink between the house and the garage. We made several attempts in the summer seasons to alleviate the problem by installing small wooden culverts under the roadway, as well as cleaning debris from the shallow drain. It did little to improve the situation – as soon as the water froze in the ditch there was no longer any drainage control.

Neither was there any sign of spring on the ocean. The white prairie of drift ice still stretched all the way to the horizon in every direction. In places where the pans of ice were not completely compressed together, ponds of blue water broke the monotonous whiteness.

At this time of year, the sheets of drift ice had reached their maximum size and thickness. On one particularly clear day, while I was watching the ice from the lighthouse, I saw a single sheet float past that was so large I was unable to see the other side even from such a high vantage point. It was easy to understand why many ships were becoming stuck in the ice. Sometimes the pressure of the moving ice field would crush a vessel, sinking it before help could arrive. On the 17th of March, 1957, we listened to our marine radio as the drama unfolded when a sealing vessel suffered just such a fate. All of the crew survived, because they had sufficient time to abandon the ship and get out onto the ice floes before the boat sank.

The first robins herald the beginning of spring for most people. Dad looked for something a little different. For him, spring began when he sighted the first sealing ship making its way past the island, heading west to intercept the seal herds in the Gulf of St. Lawrence. Many more ships would follow in the days to come, all heading for the same destination.

Just sixty miles toward the west, in an area south of the Magdalen Islands, nature was creating a miracle on the ice. Thousands of Harp seals that had migrated down from the Arctic Ocean were giving birth to their young on the ice floes. These newborn seals (known as pups) were the objects of the seal hunt.

Timing is very important, for the seal hunters must arrive at the herd when the pups are most vulnerable as well as most valuable. The mother seal will feed her young for only about two weeks. Then she abandons them, leaving them to fend for themselves. When the hunters arrive shortly thereafter, the pups are still too young to fear or sense danger, and have not yet learned how to swim. Even if they could swim, there is usually no open water into which to escape.

There is a greater demand in the fur industry for the pelts of newborn seals, as opposed to slightly more mature animals. The baby seals are known as "whitecoats" because of their fluffy white fur. After a few weeks the seals shed this coveted coat of white in exchange for one that is coarser, shorter and silvery grey. When this occurs, the seals become less valuable. They are also more active and alert, making the hunt much more difficult.

Most of the killing took place on the ice not far from where the whitecoats were born, well beyond our horizon. On one exceptional occasion, a sealing ship did intercept a herd of seals within our visual range. We could not see the distant seals, with their coats the same colour as the ice, but we could watch the excitement through our telescope.

It was a rather powerful telescope, and we never knew from whence it had originated. It was in the house when we arrived. Dad said it was most likely salvaged from some shipwreck. The brass tube was covered with intricately stitched leather, which in a few places had begun to unravel. Since it was much too heavy to hold up by hand, Dad drilled a hole in the top of a fence post and placed the large pivot pin of the telescope into the hole. By swivelling this apparatus on the post we could closely observe any ship that came past our island.

That day, when Dad announced that a sealing ship had stopped just off the lighthouse, I ran into the house and got the telescope. In minutes it was focussed on the ship and we could see the men climbing over the side. Once off the ship, they headed out on foot across the ice floes. In a matter of minutes the men had spread out over the ice. I had never before witnessed the seal hunt; I was confused when I saw the men apparently pounding the ice. Dad explained that the seals are struck on the head with a special club that crushes their skull, killing them instantly. I could see other men bent over, as though working on something else at their feet. I learned that these men were skinning the seals, and placing the pelts in a pile to be hoisted aboard the ship later. After each seal was killed and skinned, the hunter would take a few steps over to the next one to begin again.

Unfortunately, there is little market for the rest of the seal. Except for a few flippers that one of the hunters might take back to the ship for a treat, the carcass is discarded and left on the ice. Seal meat, which is almost black when cooked, is an acquired taste. It is a little too strong for the average palate.

We stood there beside the fence most of that afternoon, taking turns looking through the telescope. It was nearly dark when we noticed the seal hunters returning to the ship. I never knew if they had killed all of the seals in that herd or if they left a few alive to breed again another year. Due to the brutality of the hunting techniques, I was quite content to have watched it from a distance. I am sure that both Ina and my mother would have found this slaughter horrifying.

This was the only time during our stay on St. Paul Island that we saw the hunt actually being carried out. Quite often we would see the aftermath of a previous kill: shortly after the yearly hunt was over we would begin to notice bloodstained pans of drift ice floating past. Some of these ice floes were strewn with the carcasses of seals that had been stripped of their pelts, lying where they fell like casualties of some recent war. The only signs of life on the ice were crows and seagulls, buzzing around the remains in a feeding frenzy. Mercifully, after a few days, nature would sweep the last gruesome traces of the seal hunt out past the island and away from our view.

One bright Sunday morning, my father stormed into the house yelling, "Look out the window, everybody, look at the ice!"

I was still in bed, but sprung up, tore down the stairs, and raced everyone to the kitchen window. I stood there amazed, my eyes focussing on the numerous black spots that were sprinkled over the drift ice as far as the eye could see. These were Harp seals that had somehow escaped the hunt. Since it was quite late in the season, their coats had turned much darker in color.

I dressed immediately and ran outside for a closer look. It was an overwhelming scene. There were seals close to the shore, seals further out, and beyond that there were more seals. They were spread out quite evenly over the entire surface of the ice field, each pan loaded with seals, and the pans were far too numerous to count. In the distance they appeared only as black specks, as though someone had sprinkled the ice with pepper. The noise of their barking echoed through the calm morning air and the different voice tones were reminiscent of musicians tuning their instruments before a performance.

The tide was running quite strong that day and the ice was passing swiftly. The ice floes near the shore scraped and tumbled against the rocks. The many seals on board each sheet didn't seem to mind the bumpy ride. On every pan of ice one or two seals appeared to be standing guard while the rest of them looked as though they were sleeping. I chuckled as I watched these seal-laden pans go sliding past – the riders resembled contented hobos on a train bound for nowhere.

Dad, having grown up in Neil's Harbour where seal meat was a delicacy, longed for the flippers from one of those seals. He knew the dangers of venturing out on the ice in order to get one. It is extremely hazardous to walk on drift ice at any time, but to do so in such strong tide conditions would be suicidal. A person unfamiliar with the behaviour of drift ice might be tempted to take a hike out to sea on this white plain, especially on those days when it seemed to be pressed motionless against the shore.

An individual who better understands the unpredictability of drift ice knows the potential for disaster in such an expedition. Even after wind and tide have fused all of the floes of ice together, there are still quite often tiny gaps in between. The ice is also snow covered; the wind will drift snow into the gaps, creating an illusion of continuity. If an unsuspecting hiker should step into this pitfall trap he or she would suddenly find themselves looking up from beneath the ice. In the frigid water death will occur quickly and, even if they are fortunate enough to surface by locating the hole into which they fell, they will not survive unless someone is there to pull them out of the water. The ice pans project out of the water three feet or more, and cannot be scaled.

The second disastrous possibility, and the most feared, is ice separation. Either the sheets could separate from one another, or the whole field of ice could move away from the shore. This leaves the hiker stranded, and at the mercy of the wind and tide. This had been known to happen quite frequently in years gone by. Few had ever survived.

There were so many seals that I urged my father to make an effort to capture at least one of them. Then he told me about a tragedy that occurred on the Northeast on February 6th, 1846. Two assistant lighthouse keepers noticed a seal on the drift ice, and as it was a hard winter they seized the opportunity to get their hands on some fresh meat. They set off on foot across the ice floes and eventually reached the seal. A short time later wind or tide changed direction, causing the ice field to move away from the shore. The lighthouse keeper, Donald Boone, noticed the predicament of his two men, and with the help of a servant girl he launched a dory. The sun was setting as they rowed out to rescue the stranded men. None of them, including the courageous lightkeeper and servant girl, was ever seen again.

With this cautionary tale in mind, I contented myself with watching the herd of seals go safely on their way. This herd was so large that by evening there was still no end in sight, despite the rapidly moving field of ice. The following morning we discovered they had all disappeared. There was not a single seal to be seen anywhere on the floes.

On another cold morning, a few weeks later, I was again awakened by my father.

"Billy," he said, "wake up! There's a seal on a pan of ice in that little cove below the garage. Let's go get him!"

In a few minutes we were mushing through the knee-deep snow that covered the tractor trail. I stumbled and sometimes fell in a careless effort to keep pace with my father, whose long strides made it appear as though he were gliding through the drifts. Minutes later we turned off the trail and headed through the woods toward the shore. In the woods the snow was even deeper, but Dad took advantage of the steep descending grade and quickened his pace. So much snow was flying from his heels that it formed a white cloud behind him. We came out of the woods and stood on the rocks just above the ice. I could see the seal on a pan directly below.

Dad had brought only a coil of rope slung over his shoulders. It seemed odd to be hunting without a gun. The ice floe on which the seal was lying was pressed up against rocks by the pressure from the ocean. These were stable ice conditions; Dad didn't hesitate to venture out on this sheet for a few minutes.

The seal showed no signs of aggression at our approach. He merely raised his head and opened his mouth a little when my father tied the rope to his hind flippers. No doubt it would have been better had we slaughtered the seal there on the ice, but I suspect Dad wanted Ina and my mother to see a live seal. Slowly we pulled the seal up the slope and out the trail through deep snow. After much puffing and sweating we arrived at the house. Dad put the seal inside the workshop, and I ran to get Mom and Ina.

When Ina saw the seal it was love at first sight. His eyes were like black shiny saucers that seemed too large for his head. His coat was a light silvery grey, short and rather soft to the touch. He also had a few black patches here and there on his coat which eventually would have spread over his entire body. "Cute" was the only word to describe this little fellow. It is easy to see why, in later years, there would be so many groups and organizations opposed to the seal hunt.

Mom and Dad returned to the house. Ina and I played with the seal for most of the day, and even gave him a name. When my father returned later that evening we pleaded for his life and asked Dad if we could keep him as a pet. Dad explained that the seal would make a poor pet, and even though he was cute now, he would not remain that way for very long.

"A friend of mine had a tame seal when I was young," Dad said, "and it caused so much trouble that he finally had to get rid of it." Dad continued, "I'm sorry if you two have become attached to it, but I captured this seal for food, and that's what it's going to be."

When Dad pulled the seal out of the workshop, Ina left and went inside the house with Mom. Probably I should have accompanied her, but having decided that my departure would not change anything, I chose to stay until the end. I always helped my father with hunting duties and this was no time to be a wimp. But this was a most unpleasant chore.

It was all over in a split second. Dad struck the seal on the head using a ball-peen hammer and it collapsed without any further movement. Blood poured from the wound, flowed across the ice and trickled into the tiny cracks. I felt a little nauseated. The killing never seemed to upset my father. He had done this sort of thing many times before when he hunted seals during his career as a fisherman in Neil's Harbour. I also remembered this was how the seals on the drift ice were killed every year by the thousands, even hundreds of thousands. The death of things unseen and unknown trouble us little. Being face-to-face with the death of this baby seal, which we might have made our pet, was very disturbing to me.

However, I stayed and watched as Dad continued preparing the seal. He made an incision the whole length of the body and commenced to remove the pelt. Using his knife he peeled off the skin, which unrolled like a heavy blanket padded with a thick layer of blubber. Dad, unlike the commercial seal hunters, threw away the pelt and kept the meat. After the butchering was completed there was actually very little meat, since the flippers were the only edible portion of the seal.

When the meat was cooked, we all sat down to enjoy a meal of Dad's coveted seal flippers. Mom didn't care for it at all, and I didn't like the smell. I tried a small taste and quickly decided that I would have a meal of duck instead. Ina, on the other hand, refused to even try it, saying, "He was my friend for a while. I don't want to eat Charlie!"

The seal was gone, but a grim reminder of its death remained. The blood-stained patch of ice where it was butchered beside the workshop grew daily. As water from the bog above the house gently seeped down the hillside, it spread crimson around the station. Before long, there was scarcely anywhere one could walk without stepping on red ice. I was glad when spring finally came and the green grass replaced this last haunting evidence of the seal.

Dad made no effort to hunt any more seals, but we would have another rendezvous with the drift ice. When a homemaker runs out of sugar, she can usually go to the neighbour's house and borrow a cup. In March of 1959 when Mom ran out of baking powder, her closest neighbour was at the inaccessible Northeast. A message was relayed by radio telephone to Joe Mitchell, lightkeeper at the Northeast light station. Joe confirmed that he had an ample supply of baking powder and would be happy to loan us whatever we needed. Dad thanked Joe for his generosity and said he looked forward to seeing him at the first opportunity.

Dad and I had hiked to the Northeast on several occasions. The trail was difficult, even in the summer – especially the last section from Martin Powers to the tittle. Once we reached the tittle we would have to sit on the edge of the cliff and wait patiently for someone to come out of one of the lightkeeper's houses. Then we would yell to get their attention. On one of the trips we waited so long we both began to wonder if anyone that day would ever open the door and come outside. In the end, however, someone always came out. The not-yet-invented cell phone would have come in mighty handy. Once the staff at the Northeast were aware of our presence, someone would row over in a dory and pick us up.

In winter, however, with the road to Atlantic Cove impassible, walking the entire length of the island through the deep snow was not even an option. We had a small dory we had kept that winter in Jessie

Cove for duck hunting. To fetch the baking powder, Dad figured we could shovel the snow off the dory and prepare it for the trip. The motor, stored in the workshop, would not be difficult to get down to the boat. With the whole family working together, these tasks were completed in a few days and we were ready to launch. We were forced to wait until the drift ice retreated a safe distance from the shore. Then we had to hope it would remain out there long enough for us to make the journey to the Northeast.

Finally, the ice cooperated – at least partially. In a few places along the coast some of the ice stubbornly refused to disconnect from the shoreline. This remaining ice had either become grounded or frozen together and did not retreat with the rest of the field. This condition left us with several barriers of ice that extended in from the main ice field to the shore. Since there was no way around it, Dad decided that we could portage over the bands of ice.

The wind was calm when the four of us launched our boat into the pristine blue ocean. The flat water mirrored the beauty of the cloudless sky. With much grunting and puffing, we pulled the resisting dory through the snow inch by inch to the water's edge. Finally, with all hands on board, we hit the water and were on our way.

After just a few minutes, we arrived at the first ice blockade. Everyone carefully climbed out of the boat and onto the ice. Because of the extreme danger of walking on drift ice, Dad reminded us to hold onto the boat in case one of us should fall into an unseen water hole. We puffed and sweated as we dragged the dory across several hundred yards of ice. Streaks of yellow paint from the bottom of the boat coloured our trail. Singing seemed to make the work go easier, and we all began to sing one of Johnny Horton's songs, at that time at the top of the country charts. It seemed appropriate to the occasion: "When it's springtime in Alaska, it's forty below!" rang out across the ice.

The first portage was the longest, and went faster than we expected. We pushed the boat into open water once again and resumed the voyage. After several more short portages, I began to truly appreciate the joy of moving unobstructed through open water.

Once we were at the Northeast, there was no time to lose. Although the winds had remained calm, a changing tide could force the ice field back against the shore, leaving us with no open water in which to navigate. If the advancing ice floes sealed off our return route, we would be forced to abandon the boat on the nearest shore and wait until conditions improved. It is impossible for anyone other than an experienced mountain climber to hike along the rugged coastline of St. Paul's northern section when it is still cloaked in its winter apparel. The worse case scenario, other than freezing to death on the isolated coast, is being crushed by the moving ice field before reaching the safety of the shore. My father did not wish to be caught in this situation with two children and a wife who walked with a limp.

The sun was still quite high in the western sky when we departed for home. Warm tones from the evening sky reflected off the ice, painting the ice sheets with glowing hues of yellow and orange. Though the wind was still calm, I noticed some of the larger pans of ice beginning to stir, like sleeping giants awakening from an afternoon nap.

By the time we reached the halfway point, Dad noticed that the ice was slowly moving toward shore. We raced with the drift ice, our small motor running at full throttle. Just ahead, I could see one of the larger chunks advancing toward the shore as if determined to cut us off. This sheet appeared to be on a collision course with another mountain of ice, which the wind and tide had heaped high upon the end of a point. The moving mass and the fixed mountain of ice formed a massive gate that Dad would have to dash through before it smashed closed.

As we approached the giant floe, it towered over our tiny boat like a miniature iceberg. While passing through the narrow passage I chanced to look at my mother – her face was lined with tension. Dad stared straight ahead, his hand on the throttle, confident that we would win the race. My fear was of the motor quitting and all of us becoming the meaty contents of an iceberg sandwich. To our relief, we were successful in slipping through the narrow passage, but with little room to spare.

From the ice gate it was only a short run to where we would begin the last long portage. We were pleased to see that the ice conditions on the Southwest had not changed significantly since we had left. There was no longer any reason for concern, so we were able to somewhat enjoy that last grueling pull across the ice floes. Our timing could not have been better. When we finally hauled the boat out of the water it was time to attend to our nightly chore of lighting the light.

Later that evening while Mom and Dad were enjoying a game of cards, the radio was tuned to a local CBC station. Uncle Mose (Ted Russel, the Newfoundland author and storyteller) was spinning yarns about the amusing things that happened to rural Newfoundlanders in the fictitious community of Pigeon Inlet. We could often relate to many of his stories, since we lived in an environment similar to this isolated town. As I sat and listened to his many yarns, I wondered if someday he might tell a true story about a real family on a distant island who had worked so hard and risked so much for a single can of baking power.

15

Entertainment and Recreation

While Mother prepared breakfast, I ran outside and mounted our telescope on the fence post. Pointing it toward the mainland, I carefully focused it on the wide expanse of ocean that lay between. At first I could see only the bow wave, but soon the whole boat became visible. I watched it approaching through the telescope, until finally I could see it with my naked eye.

I had never before looked forward to the arrival of a fishing boat with so much anticipation. In the past, these small vessels had delivered only the mail, and perhaps one or two packages from relatives in Neil's Harbour. Sometimes there would be a few food items on board that Dad had ordered to hold us over until the supply ship arrived in September.

This was the summer of 1957, and the previous winter of illness had not yet faded from my memory. I remembered the promise Dad made to me when I returned to the island after my stay in the hospital. That promise would be fulfilled with the arrival of this boat. We raced the boat to the landing, and we were there waiting when it dropped anchor in Atlantic Cove.

Several weeks before, Dad had asked my grandfather to be on the lookout for the first litter of puppies born in the Neil's Harbour area. It really didn't matter what kind of a dog he found, since we were not interested in any of the purebred varieties. A radio message received the previous evening indicated that Grandfather had located a mongrel pup, and it would, weather permitting, arrive by fishing boat the following day. Fearing that I might not be interested in sharing the dog with my sister, Grandfather was sending Ina a small kitten. This was the same cat that later became Fluffy, the "kerosene kitty."

We sat up quite late that same evening discussing the new puppy, each of us wondering what it would be like. Dad would prefer to see what he called a "water dog," which could be used to retrieve ducks. Yet, as he pointed out, this was not that important since the device that we were using to retrieve birds was working well. Furthermore, one could not safely use a water dog along the coastline of St. Paul Island, with such vicious undertows, heavy surf and treacherous rocks. A trained and dedicated retriever will not hesitate to jump into the ocean in order to do its duty, without giving any thought to getting back to shore. Dad recalled several people who had lost their dogs under these conditions along other Cape Breton shores.

King, our first dog, was still very much alive. If my father felt any discomfort about introducing a new dog, there was no mention of that in the discussion. Probably King should have been enough pet for me, but being a wise old dog, he was more interested in the serious things of life instead of just playing around. There was little doubt that gentle King and the puppy would get along well together.

While a fisherman from the boat rowed ashore in a small dory, Ina and I stood on the rocks near the water's edge, waiting to receive our respective bundles. As soon as I took possession of my parcel, I opened it and proudly held the new pup up for everyone to see. My father carefully looked it over, and grimly made the prediction that this dog would never become a water dog. His opinion was based on his observation that most retrieving types were either black or brown, and usually had short hair. My dog was mainly white, except for his sable-coloured head, and even though he was just a pup, his hair was already quite long. It mattered little to me whether or not he ever became interested in the water; more importantly, I had something that would occupy my time and provide me with many companionable hours.

There is a certain amount of work involved with the raising of any animal. I wasted no time constructing the first thing necessary for my new pet's care. I found an old wooden crate that was about the right size, and with my father's help, built a roof over the box. Next, I cut out an opening, installed a door, and clumsily shingled both the roof and sides. Finally, I painted his name, "Prince," above the door and covered the floor with straw. I was very proud of that crude little house. The dog, however, didn't think that the house was fit for a prince. Each evening, I chased him around the yard for about an hour before capturing him and putting him in the house.

Prince grew up fast, and quickly proved Dad right. This dog viewed the ocean as something that should be avoided at all costs. No amount of rewards, persuasion, or force would change his feelings about the water. Prince's dislike for the water was more than offset by his superior intelligence. Ina and I spent many hours playing hide-and-seek; Prince wanted very much to be involved in the game. We ignored him for as long as we could, but when he kept locating the hidden person, the game was quickly ruined. With just Ina and myself on the island to play, there was no doubt that we would have enjoyed the game more with a third participant. We started to wonder if Prince could be trained to play the game with us.

Finally, we devised a plan in which the dog would always be the seeker. We knew that we could never teach him to stand in a corner and cover his eyes, but we could persuade him to leave us alone long enough to hide. This was accomplished by teaching him to run around the house on command. This enabled both of us to hide separately, while the dog was on the other side of the house. We christened the new game "Run Around the House," and Prince never grew tired of it. Even when we were not in the mood to play, and without anyone giving him the necessary command, Prince tried to get the game going himself. He would bark twice, and then race around the house. If one of us hadn't gone to hide when he came back around the corner, he would repeat the process several more times before giving up.

There are many stories that could be told about this dog and how he amazed us with his intelligence. The time that Mom saw him standing beside the hen house surpasses them all. Our first hens were given to us by the Cairn family when they left the island before the wireless station closed. These hens served us well for a few years, but they were quite old when we adopted them. At about the same time we got Prince, the hens had stopped laying.

The following summer, Dad placed an order for a dozen "ready laying hens" to be shipped out on the September supply ship. When the shipment arrived, Mom looked the birds over carefully and declared that we would soon be having eggs for breakfast again. Within an hour, we realized that the supplier could not have been more accurate in his timing. As we were loading them into the wagon for the journey up the trail, we noticed that one of the hens had already laid the first egg.

There was much excitement when we arrived at our house and prepared to unload the hens. One at a time, my father passed us the hens. Ina and I carried them over to the hen house and placed them inside the pen. Prince seemed to be even more excited about these new hens than we were. We would not know until the following day just how much he felt left out of "Operation Hen Replacement."

Early next morning, Mom heard a commotion up near the hen house. She looked out the window and promptly called us all over to be witnesses. Prince had a petrel in his mouth, holding it gently by the tail feathers. The bird was battering its wings frantically in an effort to escape. Prince was trying to push the petrel through the wire mesh into the chicken pen. We never knew where he found the bird, or how he captured it, but apparently he was determined to put this "hen" in the coop.

For me there was no better medicine than Prince. He kept me both entertained and occupied, filling in the voids of time that I had previously filled with daydreaming those deep and disturbing thoughts. I was no longer spending my free time trying to explain the unexplainable or resolve the impossible. The dog was not only a boy's best friend: this fellow was also a wonder drug.

While Ina and I spent most of our free time outside with our pets, our parents' entertainment was inside the house. Most of their enjoyment came from listening to the radio. Both of them were country music fans, and I too grew to love country music. On Saturday evenings we would all gather to listen to CJCB's top ten country hits, to hear if our favourite song had reached number one that week. On Sunday night this same station aired various comedy shows, and during these broadcasts no one was permitted to touch the dial – these were my father's favourite programs.

There were other times when the radio brought only sadness. One particular news story had my father glued to the radio for a couple of weeks. In October of 1958, the Springhill coal mine explosion rocked that small Nova Scotia town. Dad patiently waited for good news about survivors, and there was some – even miracles. But most of the news was bad. On the back cover of the station diary, Dad jotted down the grim statistics as they were being reported. At the bottom of the page on November 23rd, Dad made his final entry: "100 miners rescued and total killed 75."

Not only did we hear land tragedies reported, but because our radio receiver was equipped with a marine band, we also heard one sea tragedy as it happened. On a bitterly cold winter morning, we heard the skipper of the dragger *Blue Wave* in conversation with another vessel. *Blue Wave* was in rough seas, with freezing spray accumulating on the hull and superstructure. The massive weight of the ice on the superstructure made the boat top-heavy, and it was in danger of capsizing. The skipper ended his conversation by saying he was signing off to go outside and assist the crew with chopping off some of the ice. This was the last ever heard of *Blue Wave*. It is believed that the vessel capsized and sank; no trace of the boat or its crew of fourteen was ever found.

It could be argued that what we did on other occasions was an invasion of a man's privacy. He was transmitting on a public frequency, and did not appear to be concerned about whether or not anyone was listening. This man was a lighthouse keeper on a small island somewhere off the coast of Newfoundland. His island must have been relatively close to the shore, or at least close enough to see the light from a flashlight focused in his direction.

His only means of communicating with his family on the shore must have been both inconvenient and frustrating, but sometimes, for us, it was hilarious. The party to whom he was speaking obviously did not have a radio transmitter with which to give a voice response nor did they appear to have any knowledge of Morse code. They could only give an affirmative reply with the blink from their flashlight. Sometimes for hours the conversation would go something like this: "Did Aunt Martha get out of the hospital yet? Show us your light!" After that he might say, "I see your light, that's great. Was it her gall bladder again? Show us your light."

If he failed to see the light after a question, he would continue guessing until a bright flash indicated he was correct. Quite often, before he guessed the correct answer he had covered many humorous possibilities. He was fun to listen to on a cold winter night while we played a game of cards by the glow of an Aladdin lamp. Perhaps we were being a little insensitive by remaining on that shortwave frequency, but this man was sometimes more entertaining than many of the programs on the A.M. band. We called this broadcast "Show Us Your Light Hour."

There was also quiet time. Dad liked to read, and each year at the end of his vacation he returned to the island with a large cardboard box full of books. During those long winter days when little work could be done outside, he passed the hours reading novels. I never once saw my father sit and read; instead he chose to do it lying on his back on the old cot by the radio-telephone. I enjoyed those silent hours when I could concentrate on my school work without any distractions.

Quite often while Dad was reading and twiddling his toes, Mom tempted fate by ironing the clothes. She used a gas iron, an appliance similar in shape to an electric iron but with a gas tank mounted on the back. The tank was a shiny brass ball, about two and a half inches in diameter. When it was time to iron, Mom would carefully pour naphtha gas into this small tank and then pump it up with air using a miniature brass pump. When she was satisfied with the amount of pressure, she opened a valve under the tank while at the same time pushing a lighted match through one of the vent holes in the side of the iron. There would be a slight pop at ignition, followed by a fine blue flame visible on top of the base plate.

When fiery prongs protruded like whiskers out through the sides, Mom knew she had the iron set too high. There were also flare-ups over which she had no control, when for some reason the iron would momentarily burst into flames. When this occurred, she simply let go of the iron. The flames would settle down after a second or two, then Mom just resumed ironing. I was always amazed that she never burned her hand or caught the material on fire, though I did notice the iron's wooden handle was becoming charred black. Most of the time the iron worked well, purring away on a low flame while Mom hummed a tune.

We would have welcomed a little company to help pass those long winter evenings, but visitors were few even in the summer. No one came to call in the winter. Although we made several visits each summer to the Northeast light station, Joe Mitchell came to our house only once during the five years we spent on the island. When Joe and his family finally decided to visit us, Dad and I prepared a batch of ice cream as a special treat for our guests. Mom thought that perhaps one of the Mitchell children had spent a little too much time on the island. When my mother gave the oldest one a dish of ice cream, he quickly came back and complained about it being a little too cold. "Mrs. Budge," he said, "could you put this in the oven and warm it up a little?"

As they were leaving, Dad earnestly invited them to come again. In spite of their promises to return, this would be their only visit with us. It was difficult for them to travel up to our end of the island, and since Joe had no interest in boating and even less in walking, his options as to a mode of transportation were severely limited.

In contrast, the assistant lighthouse keepers on the Northeast did manage to visit us once or twice each year. The trip was usually motivated by the necessity to borrow some commodity of which they were in short supply. Keepers of the Northeast station had the privilege of using a Cape Cod dory, provided by the government for their use. With this boat, they could row the entire distance to our lighthouse or they could simply row across the tittle and walk the length of the island. The route chosen would depend mainly upon the weather.

In November of 1956, adverse weather forced one of the assistants to remain with us much longer than he had intended. Eric Rideout had come to the Northeast station earlier that year to serve as an assistant keeper. Rideout was a native of Neil's Harbour, our hometown. Because of this connection, by means of several relayed radio messages, he made arrangements to come to the Southwest for a short visit. It was always difficult to contact other lighthouse stations since we transmitted and received on different frequencies. Every message sent to another lighthouse had to be relayed through VCO North Sydney Marine Radio. It seemed to make our isolation even more pronounced; the government apparently had some reason to deny direct conversation among lighthouses.

It was a bitter cold afternoon when we launched our small, sawed-off dory and motored up to the Northeast. Our plans were to pick up Eric at the end of his shift and bring him up to our house. His plan was to spend the night with us and return to his station the following day. In the morning we would take him down to the landing by tractor and from there he would walk back to the Northeast. When he reached the tittle one of the crew from that station would row across and pick him up.

Eric seemed a bit reluctant to step into our small dory when we pulled up to the ramp. With the whole family on board, there was scarcely any room for him to sit. The rough water visible beyond the channel did little to ease his apprehension. En route the cold breeze made my eyes water whenever I looked forward to check our progress. Every now and then, the freezing spray from a bow wave would strike my skin, stinging as if someone had thrown a handful of coarse salt into my face. When we arrived at the landing Dad decided that the boating season was over. We stowed the dory away for the winter.

After supper it quickly became apparent that our friend was also a friend in need, but there was nothing we could do for him. He was experiencing nicotine withdrawal, caused not by choice but by circumstance. He thought that his supply of tobacco would last until the December supply ship arrived, but he had run out prematurely. Although there was no substitute available for his tobacco, he did find a replacement for cigarette paper, which he had run out of earlier. He enjoyed his last few smokes by rolling his tobacco in toilet paper and sealing the edges using canned milk for glue.

The irony of this was that an earlier mistake would have greatly paid off for my father, if only he had chosen to do nothing about it.

When we received our annual order of groceries from the ship chandler, which was our grocery store, there was an unexplained case of tobacco in the shipment. Dad later discovered that someone in the shipping department, for some unfathomable reason, had substituted a case of tobacco for a wheel of cheese. Since my father didn't smoke, and the rest of us didn't care to eat tobacco and crackers, Dad sent back the unwanted carton. If my father had known earlier about Eric's craving for this product, he could have held on to it and made a handsome profit.

Dad and Eric talked until almost midnight. Early the following morning we took him back to the landing, from where he would hike to the Northeast. The strength and direction of the wind raised the question as to whether or not it would be calm enough in the tittle to safely launch a dory in order to pick Eric up. Dad decided that the polite thing to do was to wait a few hours at the landing. If Eric did not return, we could assume that he had safely made it across the channel. We were just about to leave for home when our visitor reappeared from out of the woods.

"Too much sea in the tittle," he said. "I'll walk back and try it again tomorrow."

We took him home with us again and every morning for the next five days we drove him down to the landing for another attempt. When he left us on the sixth day and never came back, we assumed he had safely made it back to his home on the rock.

We never hiked to the Northeast as a family because there was no sure way of crossing the tittle. The boatswain chair was not replaced after the tragic death of George Gatza. We were content to take a casual Sunday afternoon walk down the trail or maybe hike along the windswept shores on the western side of the island. Quite often during the walk, Ina and I would recover a number of aluminum floats, washed ashore after becoming separated from the nets of the foreign fishing fleet.

Sunday was a day of rest and relaxation, and also a time for Christian education. Since we were unable to attend church, we always listened to the morning church services on the radio. I always found them refreshing – I particularly enjoyed the inspirational stories. On Sunday evening we would have our own worship service in the living room.

There, seated in his favourite chair, Dad would read several passages of scripture from the Bible, as well as read a story to illustrate the lesson. After we said a prayer, we ended the service by singing several old familiar hymns which seemed to fill everyone with the Spirit.

After the worship service, it was bedtime for Ina and me. As I drifted off to sleep, I could still hear bursts of laughter coming from downstairs as my parents listened to *I Love Lucy* on the radio.

16

Strangers in the Night

I partially opened my eyes. Then, clutching my pillow, I rolled over and tried to fall back to sleep. The room was still quite dark, but the first light of dawn was visible at the window. Sunrise came early in summer, and because I found it difficult to fall asleep after the sun had risen, I was most anxious to doze off while still under the vale of darkness. I adjusted the sheets and closed my eyes again.

Suddenly, I heard a noise. The sharp and distinct sound echoed throughout the house and seemed to vibrate the floor beneath my bed. Had it not been coming from within the house it could have been interpreted as a frantic knock at the door. It didn't seem possible at this early hour, since no one had yet risen. I knew it was still too dark for my father to extinguish the light. Even if someone were up, there was no logical reason for the person to cause a disturbance by hitting the wall.

A knocking sound generally means that there's someone at the door who wishes to enter. A knock on the door at this early hour would be disturbing in a populated area, but for us it was unthinkable. No one ever came to visit without first making arrangements by radio telephone. Our doors were never locked, but still most guests would knock on the outside door rather than somewhere inside the house.

In an adjacent bedroom, my parents were also awakened by the sound. My mother trembled. They had both become accustomed to hearing strange sounds in the night, but Mom was never comfortable with these unexplained disturbances. That morning she held onto my father more tightly than ever and said, "Freddy, we have to get off this island now. This time they've gone too far!"

It was not the first time that we had heard strangers in the night, but it was the first time they had ever bothered to knock. It was also unusual for them to be still lingering around at the break of dawn.

There were no obvious defects in the doors of our house, and due to the severe weather we experienced Dad inspected them regularly. All the knobs functioned correctly; when doors were closed, each bolt slipped securely into the recess of the jamb. None of our inside doors could be properly opened without someone first turning the knob.

Neither the winter gales that whistled around outside nor the strong gusts of wind that rattled the dishes in the cupboard were ever successful in opening one single door. But on calm and quiet evenings, doors would start to open. The basement door was usually the first. We would be in the living room listening to the radio. We would hear the creaking of the hinges, followed by the thud when the door came to rest against the adjacent wall. It was not a frequent event, but it happened often enough that my mother noticed specific timing: the door always opened at eight in the evening. Someone would close the door, but Dad would usually find it open when he came downstairs in the morning to light the fire. Several of our inside doors were always kept closed when not in use. Yet many times my father found them all open in the morning, as if our home had been invaded by some unwelcome visitor during the night. The outside doors always remained closed.

Even more unsettling than the basement door was the one at the base of the stairs. This door led into a small mud room at the front entrance of the house. My parents slept in the bedroom at the top of the stairs, and on numerous occasions my mother also heard the mud room door opening in the middle of the night. Dad was always willing to get up and close it, but he could never explain to my mother's satisfaction why it happened in the first place.

My father did not believe in ghosts. He was, therefore, determined to solve the riddle of the doors once and for all. He planned to build two simple hardwood latches, install them on the doors, and end the mysterious disruptions in the night. When Mom heard about his plan she was livid.

"I won't allow you to do that, Freddy," she said. "Right now I only *think* this house is haunted. If you latch those doors like that and they still come open, I will *know* that the house is haunted!" Due to Mom's reluctance to confront the unknown, the ultimate latch test was never carried out.

We were not the first family to experience strange phenomena in this house. Prior to coming to St. Paul Island, my mother spoke with a gentleman who at one time had served as a radio operator at Atlantic Cove. During his term on the island, he once visited with the lightkeeper on the Southwest and stayed with him several nights. On the last night of his visit, he swore that he had an encounter with the supernatural that was so frightening he would never again spend as much as one single night inside that house. He was determined to share his experience with my mother, prior to our moving to St. Paul Island, but she wisely refused to hear his story. She felt that whatever tale he was about to tell her was probably nonsense, and would only cause her to be unnecessarily nervous when this same house would become our home.

Whether or not our place was haunted, the stage was set for the superstitious when the house was built in 1916. During construction, builders claimed to have unearthed human bones while excavating for the basement. This was highly probable because of the many unmarked mass graves of shipwreck victims on the island. A few hundred feet to the west of where our house was built, the survivors of the shipwreck *Jessie* made their makeshift shelter, only to starve to death during the winter of 1825. It would be no surprise if the bodies of these victims rested in the area that later became the basement of our house.

Was there some kind of scientific explanation for the way in which our inside doors came open during the night, or had we received a visit from the spirits of the departed? Disturbed bones in the basement would explain why that door always opened first.

There were other unsettling nocturnal events in addition to the unexplained door openings. Sometimes in the middle of the night, sounds like pieces of wood being thrown at the sides of the house interrupted our sleep. We tried to determine the cause of these strange thumping sounds, but never came up with an explanation. My father's inability to explain or eliminate these mysterious sounds exacerbated my mother's fears.

On one occasion, shortly after midnight, my parents were lying in bed when they heard noises in the living room. These noises they could identify, or at least they thought they could. It was a few days after Christmas, and as they were drifting off to sleep they heard the sound of ornaments falling off the tree. They could even hear the telltale sound of the bells rolling across the floor and bouncing along as they tumbled over their stems. This was easily identified as the work of Ina's cat, Fluffy. "Fluffy is certainly wound up tonight. We'll sure have a mess to clean up in the morning," Mom said, as she drifted off to sleep.

The next morning Dad arose early as usual for the purpose of extinguishing the light, and it was fortunate for my mother that he came downstairs alone. As he stood there in the living room and gazed upon the tree, he was puzzled to find that none of the decorations had been disturbed. There were no ornaments on the floor, and no sign of any broken bells anywhere in the house. Dad knew there was no way he could have misinterpreted the noises he heard the night before. Yet there was no evidence to suggest that the tree or anything on it had been touched.

Maybe someone else was in the living room that night, someone who could have replaced the ornaments on the tree. Could it have been the infant ghosts of young children who perished on some ancient shipwreck? It would seem almost typical that they would have more interest in playing with the ornaments than with the modern gifts that were still lying under the tree. Among these gifts was a guitar that I couldn't play. Had the strangers chosen to play a few chords on this instrument, there is little doubt that Mom and Dad would have sung a different tune as they lay in bed and listened! Whatever it was, Mom would never know the truth about the Christmas tree or the ornaments until after we had moved from St. Paul Island. At the time, Dad simply claimed that he picked up the bells and redecorated the tree after he returned from the lighthouse.

The morning that I heard the knocking downstairs, Dad hadn't yet gone out to the light. As I listened, it became louder, as if it were desperately trying to attract our attention. When my father left the bedroom to investigate, Mom was certain that this would be the morning that all speculation would end, and Dad would finally come face to face with someone from the spiritual realm. My father, not believing in ghosts, was not so sure. He was quite certain that he would find nothing downstairs at all, but felt that his presence would at least cause the disturbance to cease.

To his surprise, the intruder was waiting for him when he stepped into the kitchen. The tall, thin figure standing beside the window was none other than my grandfather, quite alive and in the flesh. He had left Dingwall by fishing boat in the early hours of the morning, and it was still dark when they arrived at St. Paul Island. At first light, one of the fisherman rowed him ashore at Jessie Cove, leaving him with only a short, strenuous hike up to our house.

For a moment I listened intently to the conversation downstairs, thinking that perhaps some serious marine incident had brought this early morning visitor to our door. It required only a few seconds for me to identify that familiar, loud and friendly voice. I sprang out of bed and flew down the stairs with such haste that my mother probably thought I had seen the ghost. I rushed to my grandfather, and after a long embrace, began to talk. I talked for some time, since there was so much to tell.

I gave Grandfather a tour of our light station after breakfast, first showing him the lighthouse while explaining in detail how the equipment operated, and how we lit the light every evening. I pointed out the heavy weights hanging from the cable and told how it was my job to winch them up each evening. I even demonstrated my chore by turning the crank and watching the cable accumulating on the drum. I must have been an excellent guide, or my grandfather was a good listener, because he asked very few questions at the end of the lighthouse tour.

At the garage, Grandfather's trust in me would be put to the test. He stood there smiling as he watched me back the tractor outside, but when I asked him to sit in the driver's seat and come with me for a ride, his smile suddenly disappeared. I probably didn't inspire his confidence when I added, "You sit in the driver's seat, Grandfather. I don't need it, because I drive standing up!"

For most people, an invitation for a 'Sunday drive' would not require putting their life in the hands of a nine-year-old child, especially when the adult is seated in the driver's seat. But for Grandfather it was different. He had never owned a car, nor had he ever learned how to operate any kind of motor vehicle. One could only imagine his trepidation, as he sat helplessly on the seat while I stood in front of him, jauntily operating the machine and pointing out the sights as we motored along the treacherous trail. However, Grandfather slowly relaxed as he became more sure of my driving skills. We turned near the bluff and went back to the station.

The final stop in our tour of the station property would be the one of most interest to my grandfather. In a spare upstairs bedroom, Dad had allowed me to set up a very primitive woodworking shop. My tools were limited to a handsaw, a coping saw, a hammer and a chisel. I had already completed several simple projects, and some of these crude creations were displayed in the house when Grandfather arrived.

The most noteworthy of my creations were two primitive tables that were used as school desks, one for my sister and one for myself. I built them using recycled lumber we found near the wireless station after it had closed. This material had been previously used on an exterior structure and what little paint remained on each piece was peeling off in large grey and white flakes. I sawed and nailed the pieces together and although it was not a work of art, it stood upright and provided a level surface on which to write. I was quite proud of the finished product, in spite of the fact that a pencil could almost fall through the cracks between the boards in the desk top.

For the most part, the only stock that I could use for my projects was a long pine board about ten inches wide. When Grandfather arrived, all that remained of my stock was a short piece, and it was lying across an old wooden box which served as my work bench. My father allowed me to use one such board per year, which he selected from a limited supply of government lumber that had been intended for use in the upkeep of the station.

Grandfather was very proud of my accomplishments, in spite of my crude workmanship. For my most challenging project I would need his help. Hanging on the wall was a pattern for the Buckingham Palace guard that Earl O'Halloran had left me the previous year. Because of the difficult cuts and sharp curves that would be required to complete this project, I had not even attempted it.

I realized that with Grandfather's knowledge and woodworking skill we could easily complete this project. I watched with amazement as he made all those fancy cuts using only a handsaw. Of course he had me make some of the simple cuts and in a very short time it was ready to be sanded and painted. This I managed to accomplish on my own, and when it was completed it looked very much like the one in the picture. This particular piece remained in the family for many years, and although Grandfather would often brag about how Billy did this when he was only nine years old, I am sure that most people knew better.

My grandfather enjoyed his visit and remained with us for more than a week. He left with a much better understanding of the bleak and lonely place that we called home. In his mind he could now form a real picture of where and how we lived, instead of creating a fictitious scene in his imagination. If he had any emotional reaction to his first visit to the island he kept it to himself; he was not one to reveal much excitement. However, he had visited during the summer, when the island was clothed in the lush greenery of that season. He couldn't begin to imagine what it would be like to live there in the harsh solitude of winter.

I don't recall if we ever had another knock at the door, but the strangers in the night would continue to come and go. If they were indeed ghosts, they were a shy lot, for they never chose to present themselves to any of our family. So what if they forgot to close a few doors after a night of romping and playing downstairs? We should have been happy for the opportunity to allow them some comfort after what must have been miserable deaths.

17

Final Thoughts
and a
Reluctant Farewell

By February 1960, we had adapted so well to our circumscribed life on St. Paul that any other way of life was unimaginable. We had experienced five years of island life, so much of my and Ina's childhood that we could say we grew up there. There was little in this small world that I would have changed even if I could, although there were times when the realities of daily life were somewhat less than paradisaical. It was perfect only in its imperfections: there were always problems to be solved and challenges to be met that the rest of the world could never know. It was the satisfaction derived from doing the impossible with next to nothing that made life interesting. If there was any reason for a change, I couldn't see it. But I may have been a little shortsighted.

I saw only the excitement of a winter storm, on those days when nature unleashed its fury. Ofttimes I would stand beside the lighthouse, holding onto my cap as I leaned forward against the howling wind, freezing spray pelting my face. Through squinted eyes I watched mountainous seas pound the rocks below, blasting columns of spray high into the air. Soft clouds of sticky froth rose out of the foamy turmoil and fled before the wind. These lathery clumps then danced their way up the grassy slope and flew past our house to rejoin the ocean on the other side of the island. It was a beautiful sight to behold while standing safely on the shore, but the sailors of long ago saw it differently, watching a similar scene from the deck of their disintegrating ship.

On stormy nights, I dozed off to the sounds of thundering surf, better than listening to the dynamic notes of Beethoven's Fifth Symphony, and awakened to the peaceful silence of the morning after. By dawn the angry waves would have begun to relax, and the sun would be peeping through the broken clouds. Nature's grand exhibition was over. I always felt she gave her best performance when the weather was at its worst.

I often beheld the beauty of the early morning sky, its hues of mauve and purple light preceding the rising of the sun. Suddenly, with a flash of radiant orange, the sun would peek above the horizon and rise slowly out of the sea. In the evening, the sun returned to its nest in the sea on the opposite side of the island, slipping beneath the waters of the Gulf of St. Lawrence. Layered clouds of crimson red hovered above the scene and lingered there in the darkening sky until the stars came out and took their place.

There were also the cold moonlit nights of winter. The full moon cast its shimmering gleam across the lonely sea, for there was little else on which it could shine. The beam of light sweeping from the lighthouse paled in comparison to the brilliance of the moon and seemed lost in its superior glow. Sometimes I would sit and view the moon through our powerful telescope, marvelling at the lunar landscape. The breathtaking close-up appeared too awesome to be real.

I enjoyed our rare guests. We welcomed everyone, and it did not matter who they were or from whence they came. One thing was always certain: there would be plenty of laughter and excitement around the dinner table as tales were told, and jokes and news exchanged. Mom went out of her way to make the visitor feel at home. Seldom did anyone leave our house without first experiencing some unusual or amusing event that they would always remember.

Another rare event about which I could not contain my enthusiasm was the annual arrival of the supply ship. Besides all the fresh food and vegetables in the shipment, there were also a few special treats. Even though many of these items were inclined to spoil quickly, Dad felt that we should, at least occasionally, enjoy the sort of treats other children could purchase daily at a corner store.

After the boat pulled away from the island, we were left with the backbreaking job of transporting everything up to the station. It usually required more than a week to haul home the cases of food, barrels of oil and the many bags of coal. It was strenuous work, yet I felt a little disappointed after we had made the final run.

There were some surprises, like the time a huge boulder fell on the tractor trail and blocked the road. It was so large that it could not be moved with the tractor or any other equipment that was available. It was impossible for us to build a detour around it, due to the high bank on one side of the road and the sudden drop-off on the opposite side. The only option we had was to drive over the rock. After shovelling and hauling countless wagon-loads of gravel, we buried the rock and completed a mini overpass. Our problem-solving skills were constantly being tested and honed by such challenges.

It became evident after our second year on the island that the population of rabbits was steadily declining. During our third winter, the situation rapidly deteriorated. We would quite often find rabbits frozen to death in a sitting position under a tree. For some reason, the few remaining survivors sought refuge underneath the tractor garage. We fed them regularly with table scraps, and improved their shelter by sealing off some of the larger openings underneath the garage. But still they continued to die. I constructed a wooden cage for the last two rabbits and brought them into the house, hoping that the warmth would give them a new lease on life. However, they seemed determined to die. After only a few days in the house they were both dead. Perhaps their deaths were caused by some disease, or it may have been part of the mystery of St. Paul Island. Even this failed conservation effort didn't dampen our spirits because we could take comfort in the knowledge that we had made a sincere effort.

We enjoyed boating and fishing from spring through early fall, and duck hunting occupied our time throughout the winter. Since there were no game wardens or fisheries officers, there was no need for any licenses. Only the weather and our respect for nature's time to reproduce would dictate an end to each season. This was indeed an unusual privilege and, in my limited perspective, I thought that it would last forever.

My father, on the other hand, saw things from a different view. In spite of the fact that he also shared with me in the excitement and freedom of living in a private world, he saw the need for change. Some of these changes would have to come quickly in order to avoid serious problems that would certainly have arisen had he done nothing. It was during the winter of 1960 that he decided to take the action.

Our schoolwork was his main concern. At the time I was completing grade six, and the lessons were becoming increasingly difficult. With his limited education, my father knew that soon he could be of little help should I have difficulty understanding the assignments. Although my father lacked a high-school education, he was an intelligent man and well read. His teaching techniques, however, left something to be desired. He had little patience for teaching any subject, and for history and English literature, he had none at all. I was always reluctant to ask him for help with these lessons because of his negative and punitive attitude. If I chose to continue without a clear understanding, and completed the work incorrectly, the situation would become much worse. Dad would find the mistake later, and before that day ended I would deeply regret my decision to continue without help.

He usually began his lecture seated in his favourite armchair. Although I was seated at my desk right beside him, his articulation was loud enough to be heard across an entire auditorium. The lesson was taught with angry words and delivered in a harsh, gritty and irritating voice. He sank further into his chair as the lecture proceeded, becoming progressively louder and more overbearing. Every now and then he forcefully jabbed his finger toward me, and pounded on my desk with his fist as if trying to literally drive the point home. Then, he would ask me a question, a question far too risky for me to venture to answer. The consequences would be dire should I respond incorrectly, and were the same every time.

I knew my answer was wrong if he stood up. A hard slap to the back of my head from his big right hand confirmed I had answered incorrectly. In the next instant, the text book that I had been holding was ripped out of my hands and flung violently across the living room floor. I walked across the room and picked up the book, as I was ordered to do. Then I returned to my desk and was expected continue with the lesson. But it is difficult to think while under fire, and I would inevitably utter another wrong answer, starting the cycle all over again.

Finally, I would be unable to stand the tension and blows anymore. Tears would begin streaming down my face and dripping onto my notebook. This transformed the writing on the paper into inky blotches and the pages started to dissolve. This incensed my father even more.

My timid mother, seated in the same room, tried to show no emotion and continued with her knitting. I could see that she was upset, but also unable to make any effort to intervene. When she began to feel as though the "lesson" might never end, she came over to Dad and softly suggested, "Freddy, don't you think you guys should put this away tonight, and maybe work on it again tomorrow?"

"Hell no, Edith," he'd say. "I intend to sit here all night if that's how long it takes me to beat this into his head!" Still, eventually, he would usually take Mom's advice. Then the following day, we would complete the lesson calmly.

My father did not lose his temper with me this way every day, but it happened too often. The following year would be even more troublesome, for we could look forward to algebra, and the French language would be introduced as a subject. This was a language that Dad could neither understand nor speak. He knew that it could never be properly taught without the services of a knowledgeable French-speaking tutor.

Unlike other correspondence students, we had a major disadvantage due to our extreme isolation. The examiners who monitored our progress were very helpful. They not only corrected our mistakes but at the same time they would demonstrate the proper method of completing the exercise. Under normal circumstances this would have been sufficient, but due to the irregularity of the mail, the instructions were seldom received in time to prevent mistakes from recurring.

From the date we began school in September, until the supply ship arrived in December, the mail would have been sent out and received several times. The frequency of mail delivery was made possible through the courtesy of fishermen who happened to be fishing in the area. Between the months of January and April there would be no mail service at all, but schoolwork had to continue uninterrupted. When the drift ice finally left in the spring and the first ship arrived, we mailed ashore four months of lessons to be corrected. At the same time, we received the marks for work completed back in December. It was indeed a sickening feeling when you realized that you had made a grievous error earlier in the school year that you unknowingly repeated throughout the winter, and then to look up to see the ship sailing off with those same mistakes. In that situation one could only hope for a sympathetic examiner.

One particular examiner, who was not very sensitive, apparently had some difficulty grasping the uniqueness of our situation, and as a result, was given a harsh lesson in geography by my father. It was probably caused by that continuous mistake syndrome, occurring in a series of lessons that annoyed this lady and prompted her to write an acerbic note at the bottom of one of my papers. She explained that if each lesson was mailed in weekly as is intended with correspondence courses, then early correction would eliminate repetitious errors. She continued by saying that she would no longer accept our policy of withholding several months of lessons and sending them all in at once. She ended on a threatening note, saying that this was our last warning and any further disregard of instructions would not be tolerated.

My father, with his abrupt and outspoken attitude, took pen in hand and fired off a scathing letter to this unsuspecting woman. He told her about St. Paul Island and the mail service, in much the same way as I have explained except that he used more colourful language. He ended his note by saying that he would be only too glad to give her the lessons one at a time if she'd care to drop by each week and pick them up.

Deep down inside, however, my father realized that this lady had a point. He knew that both Ina and I would soon require a more standard education, which could only be achieved in a normal classroom with licensed teachers. I could only hope that these teachers would never use my father's technique when they taught their lessons. I do, however, feel that Dad recognized his teaching limitations and decided that our circumstances needed to be changed.

The wonder, the mystery, the solitude and the beauty of St. Paul Island had cast its spell on my mother as well as the rest of us. Yet, through it all, she maintained her grip on reality. In the back of her mind was the constant fear of having to contend with a sudden injury or illness, and what might happen in the long hours or days to the affected family member before he/she received professional medical attention. She had already experienced a winter of sickness and had seen the inadequacies of the communication system, as well as those of a transportation service totally at the mercy of the vagaries of the weather.

For the most part, my mother's love for the island overpowered her fears, and conceivably she could have continued to live there as long as my father wished to, but she was not a selfish person. She saw her children growing up in an environment that deprived them of all the amenities that normal children take for granted. She felt that Ina and I had lived long enough in a world without friends, schools, churches and sports activities. Therefore, my mother arrived at the same conclusion as my father – it was finally time for us to re-enter society.

They were both wrong, because for me, it was already too late. My life had been moulded and shaped by the powerful gravity of a different world – a world from which I could not easily break free. In the course of five years, time had spun a web of independence that held me apart, and because I had been hypnotized by its serenity I had no desire to escape. It had not been just five short years as those experienced in later life, but instead they were the long, slow and influential years of youth. But the die had been cast (although to me it didn't seem right) and we would soon leave St. Paul Island forever.

Over the radio telephone, Dad received a list of lighthouses that required replacement lightkeepers. The various stations were scattered all along the shores of Nova Scotia. My parents were eager to select a suitable location and apply for a transfer. Dad pulled an atlas off the shelf, and with the list in hand, seated himself beside my mother at the table. A lamp flickered between them as they studied the possibilities, straining their eyes in an effort to locate the various places on the map. I took no part in the discussion, and would have been quite content had they found nothing satisfactory at all.

Finally, they narrowed down the list and focussed their attention on two possibilities. One of these was Ingonish Island. It was located just six miles from Neil's Harbour and less than half a mile from the shore. The narrow body of water that separated the island from the village of Ingonish was calm, except during severe storms. There was even a boat dock strategically located on the mainland, insomuch that it was directly across the water from the island. Most importantly, the school was located a short distance from the wharf.

At first glance, it appeared to be the perfect location. We would not have to surrender our island status, yet it was close enough to the shore to commute back and forth to school each day. Dad figured on using his small boat to ferry us across the channel to the wharf; from there we would walk to school. In the evening he would return to pick us up.

It was an excellent plan but weather was a major glitch. If there was too much surf on the island's small beach, a boat could not be safely launched. Should a storm develop during the day, Ina and I would have to spend the night at someone's house. In the winter, we would still have to deal with the drift ice, which could fill the passage for weeks and make the crossing too dangerous to undertake. Dad suggested that during the worst part of winter it might be better if Ina and I stayed at a boarding house somewhere in town. Mom, on the other hand, would not agree to any arrangement that prevented her children from returning home at the end of each school day. In the end, they both decided that Ingonish Island was unacceptable. They began to study the last option.

The other possibility was a lighthouse located almost two hundred miles away on the eastern shore of the Nova Scotia mainland. It was situated on a point at the harbour entrance to the tiny fishing village of

Port Bickerton. The light station was equipped with a fog horn, so there would also be an assistant keeper to share the workload. The site was located one and a half miles from the village and was accessible by means of a rugged trail along a rocky beach. The road was a rough one but a least there was no water between the lighthouse and civilization.

The educational facilities were appealing as well. Ina, who was entering grade six, would attend an elementary school in the village. As for me, I would begin grade seven at a junior high school, about twenty miles away in the town of Sherbrooke. This would involve a daily commute by school bus.

When Dad finally received all the essential information about Port Bickerton and he and my mother had pored over the material, they made their decision. Almost immediately Dad forwarded an application for the new position by means of a radio message to the Department of Transportation.

The answer came quickly – even more quickly than my father had anticipated. The affirmative response meant that our time on St. Paul Island was rapidly coming to an end. We were further advised to be packed and ready to leave by mid-April. The approaching deadline left us with only a few weeks to prepare for moving day.

My excitement and enthusiasm were subdued compared to my reaction when similar news was received only five years before. This time I couldn't stand upon a rock and see our destination from a nearby point, as I had done with my grandfather in Neil's Harbour. Neither did we have any photographs of our new lighthouse station, so that I could at least study them and picture myself in the scene. The only thing I knew for sure was that we were moving much farther away than I had ever been before.

However, there was something even more frightening to me than the uncertainty of the new location. There would be people – lots of people, and none of them would be my friends or relatives. Even worse was the thought of going off to school on a bus filled with strangers. I expressed these fears to my mother and she tried to comfort me by saying that many of these children would become my friends after I became acquainted with them. I told her that I was perfectly happy living here in my own little unpeopled world. Mom tried with various arguments to convince me that this move would be for the better. I remained sceptical and simply continued to help my father with the packing.

Packing was much easier this time because my father had kept most of the cartons and crates. Sadly, there was one item that we had brought to the island that would not be making the return trip. King, our long-time friend and faithful servant, was no longer with us. His unusual but exciting life had come to an end only a few months before.

Although he was not a duck retriever there was never any doubt that he loved the water. Whenever we ventured out to sea in the dory, King always swam behind the boat, following us until he grew tired, whereupon he would return to the landing. Prince, being afraid of the water, was content to remain on the shore and bark until he was rejoined by King. At the end of a day of work fishing it was a pleasure to see the dogs waiting there, their tails wagging.

Perhaps it was his age, but something caused him to become disoriented one day, and King did not return to the landing after his usual swim. When we returned to shore, Dad was most upset to see only Prince waiting on the shore and no sign of King. As soon as our boat was hauled up and secured to the ramp we began a full scale search for the missing dog. We checked the many tiny coves along the shore, which he may have entered and then climbed out of the water. It was quite possible that he had become trapped on a rocky ledge beneath some cliff that he was unable to scale. We continued to search until dark, but there was no sign of him anywhere; neither was there any barking in response to our calls. We returned the following day in hopes of having better luck but when we failed to find any trace of him again, Dad gave him up for dead.

On the third day the sea was exceptionally calm and my father suggested we search from the water. We launched the boat and rowed quietly along the coast while looking deep into those narrow coves that one could not see into from the shore. Not far from the landing we entered a narrow inlet with a very steep, overhanging cliff on either side. As we passed through, the scene gave me the eerie feeling of entering a cave. I peered ahead into the partial darkness – the quicker we were able to determine that there was nothing there, the quicker we could leave. Suddenly, to my surprise and my father's delight, King was standing upon a ledge of rock and wagging his tail. He had been trapped in there with no way out other than to swim, and I suspect that after having been exhausted when he first arrived, he lacked the necessary courage to leave. Any remaining strength must have been expended by barking, for he only managed to whisper a bark when we rescued him. Needless to say, there was a happy reunion when we returned home with the missing family member.

This incident only served to show that King was growing old and his days were numbered. In fact, he spent most of his time lying on the step and he never chased the tractor anymore. I had noticed that chunks of hair were always falling from his coat and he had difficulty getting to his feet. Although he wasn't whimpering or otherwise indicating discomfort, Dad suspected that he might be suffering.

Early one morning, when I stepped outside I noticed that he wasn't in his usual place. The first thing I did was to question my mother about his disappearance, and as all good mothers do – she lied! She explained that when animals become ill they usually go away to find a private place to die. I hoped that King would change his mind and come home again, but he never did.

The truth about what actually happened to King was, wisely, withheld from me. Without the services of a veterinarian, it fell to my father to end his dog's suffering. Earlier that morning Dad coaxed King to take a short hike with him to the edge of the cliff. In a scene not unlike that in Walt Disney's *Old Yeller*, Dad raised his shotgun and ended the life of King with a single shot to his head. In a fitting farewell ceremony for a dog who loved the water, he was given a burial at sea by sliding his body over the cliff and into the ocean. It must have been a heart-wrenching experience for my father, but I never once saw him cry. He had said his goodbye to King. Very soon we would say goodbye to St. Paul Island.

We would leave our craggy post with the satisfaction of having performed a valuable service, and having done it well. There were no shipwrecks to report, neither was there ever a demand for us to take part in any dramatic rescues. Unlike our predecessors, who were frequently witness to disaster and tragedy, we saw mostly efficiency and routine. We had kept our light burning through winter storms when its beam was cut short by blinding snow. We had kept it flashing through freezing rain, my father labouring in the dark and cold for endless hours pounding ice off the cable to free the rotating mechanism. On clear nights its beam swept unobstructed across the cold and lonely sea, a reliable comfort for perplexed sailors searching for a guiding light.

Only once did we come close to knowing the desperate stress so familiar to the lifesaving sentinels of the previous century. It was late on a fall evening, with a clear sky and a calm sea. Mom, alone in the living room on the lighthouse side of our home, heard a noise.

"Freddy," Mom called, "I think something just exploded up in the lighthouse."

Dad, dropped what he was doing and rushed outside. From the lighthouse he could see a large ship beneath the cliff, so close that he could almost jump on board. He could clearly hear the panicked voices of her crew as they tried to prevent their vessel foundering. Her engines were running full speed astern in a desperate attempt to cease forward motion and back safely away from the treacherous shore. They were rewarded for their efforts for within a few minutes the ship sailed away unscathed, its engines pounding, probably much like the hearts of the frightened sailors on board. We never learned if this near mishap was caused by human error or by equipment problems on board, but no doubt someone on watch must have seen our light at the last possible moment and saved the day. If our light had prevented only one shipwreck, or saved only one life, then we had not served in vain.

The process of preparing for the move took a couple of weeks. Load by load, Dad and I hauled all our belongings down to the landing. The final days of our island life slipped by, with little time available for me to think about a life after St. Paul. For me, the excitement of the moment overshadowed the fact that we were leaving forever. I found the uncertain future wasn't something I wanted to think about.

Almost as quickly as the government approved my father's transfer, they found a replacement lightkeeper. The move for the new lightkeeper would be a short one: he was already working as an assistant at the Northeast lighthouse. He was a retired fisherman turned lightkeeper, and other than his wife he had no immediate family. We knew him well: Wilson Ingraham, the same man who nearly rode off to glory with his crew in our runaway wagon the day the hitch pin popped out. There was no doubt that he would make an excellent replacement, as he was both a hard worker and a trustworthy individual.

Moving day arrived, the last few items were tossed aboard the wagon for the final run – yet I had still not come to grips with the situation. Mom and Ina climbed into that old reliable box seat on the back of the tractor and prepared for their last ride down the trail. A tear rolled slowly down my mother's cheek as she turned to look back at the house in which we had shared so many special moments over the years. It had not only served as our home – it was a church, a hospital, a school and a recreation centre. My mom, the homemaker who tended the building and created the caring atmosphere within it, would miss it most of all.

I never looked back when we left the station. It seemed to me like we were leaving for just another short vacation. A few hundred yards up the trail we rumbled over a dilapidated bridge. Earlier in the year, Dad had said that we would be installing a new beam and rebuilding the top in the spring, and I couldn't wait to get started. Just beyond the bluff we plunged into a huge hole on one side of the road. I recalled that in order to repair it we would have to haul and shovel many wagonloads of gravel. Outside the cove the supply ship that would take those responsibilities away from me forever was waiting for us. In my heart, the road and that work were still mine.

At the landing, I stood at a safe distance and watched the reverse operation of what I had observed five years before. Piece by piece, our furniture was hoisted up with the boom, then swung out over the cliff and lowered into the landing barge below. In the distance, the *Edward Cornwallis* was anchored in calm water on the inside edge of an endless field of drift ice. It was as though nature had moved the ice offshore just far enough for us to load our possessions and board the ship. Only an occasional sheet of ice still lingered in the cove, casting its reflection on a glassy silver sea. The scene was reminiscent of the day we launched the dory and journeyed up the coast to the Northeast light station to borrow the can of baking powder. I longed for an opportunity to repeat that adventurous trip. The voyage we were about to undertake would forever deprive me of the chance of realizing that dream.

Finally, the last load was stowed aboard the launch. There was little time to dwell on the past. At the time there was the excitement of the present, and I was caught up more in the act of moving than the move itself. Then slowly, in single file, we made our way down the steep incline to the water's edge. The last few feet were the worst for Mom. Dad held her hand as she stumbled over the icy rocks. The crew helped us all aboard and as the launch pulled away from that old familiar cliff we said a reluctant farewell to St. Paul Island.

We made our way toward the waiting ship, like a family walking away from the grave of a loved one. Mom was nestled among some cardboard boxes near the stern, a faraway look upon her face. She was holding my sister in her arms, and Ina, who seldom showed any emotion, seemed to be struggling within, as she clutched her kitten tightly. Dad chatted quietly with one of the crewmen while I sat in the bow holding Prince.

Once on board the ship we departed immediately. The Captain came to our cabin and extended an invitation to my father and me to join him on the bridge, where we could observe the boat breaking a passage through the drift ice. I watched with excitement as the bow struck the smaller sheets. I noticed when they rolled over from the force of the impact they were more cubed-shaped than flat. This ship was not only a supply vessel but an icebreaker, designed to navigate through heavy ice. Whenever we rammed into large sheets the ship slid partially out of the water, almost stopping, until its massive weight finally cracked the ice, and we charged through the watery fissure that opened ahead of us. In this manner the icebreaker continued to make slow progress until at last I saw that the distant mainland was gradually increasing in size.

Then I turned around and looked back. St. Paul Island was shrinking in our wake, slowly settling beneath an horizon of jagged ice. It would soon be gone from my view, but never from my soul. Even though we were leaving the island behind, I knew I was taking some of it with me. Even now, when alone in a quiet place, that sense of security and happiness from my solitary St. Paul Island childhood returns.

It was too late in the year to begin school when we arrived at our new lighthouse at Port Bickerton. I finished my last few remaining lessons by correspondence in the usual manner. I spent most of that summer exploring the new territory, but made little effort to make new friends in the nearby village. I figured that there would be plenty of time for socializing when school started again in the fall.

That first day of school was a very traumatic experience. I waited for the school bus at the nearest stop, and when it pulled up I climbed on board. For a long moment, I stood there gazing into the faces of the strangers, who were in turn staring at me. These were the children of a small village where everyone knew everyone else, but I didn't know them and they didn't know me. Perhaps I could have introduced myself, but no one seemed very interested. Furthermore, if I spoke at all, I could find myself in the position of trying to explain why I, at the age of twelve, had never gone to school before.

When we arrived at the high school in the village of Sherbrooke, things went from bad to worse. We stepped off the bus and I joined the hoards of other children already swarming around in front of the school. At the sound of the buzzer I followed the stampede into the gymnasium. There we awaited the formation of the various classes as the groups of names were read from a prepared list. As I sat and listened for my name to be called, I glanced around the large room. It was wall-to-wall people. For a moment I forgot what I had studied about population and felt that everyone in the world must have assembled in this one room. I was surrounded by 318 energetic school children and it was the first time in my life that I had ever been lonely.

My mind wandered back to that island across the sea where life seemed so orderly and predictable, the only factors to deal with being those involved in daily survival. I knew that St. Paul Island had been Hell to the ancient mariners, and to most it was a place to be shunned, but for me it was a Paradise lost. I could see nothing here for me, and even imagined that if I dropped dead, these people would merely step over me as they continued on toward their destinations. The polished floors, the neat rows of varnished desks, the basketball hoops, and the smiling teachers – I would gladly trade them all for a chance to sit at my own crude desk beside the window and watch the distant ships slipping along the horizon.

As if to add to my feeling of dislocation and anonymity, they never did call out my name on that first day of school. Since my father had not made previous arrangements, the school was not aware of my presence. Being the only one left in the gymnasium after all the names had been called, I had little choice but to follow the last student to his assigned class. I found a seat, sat down, and waited for the worst.

What happened after that is another long story, but eventually the discrepancies were resolved and I found myself a place in grade seven. I was not moved back any grades as some people had predicted but neither was I moved forward. Very quickly, I became an average student and did well academically but it would take years to completely adjust to society. Like a tree that continues to grow crookedly after the twig has been bent, I would always bear the mark of St. Paul Island.

After finishing high school, I became a service technician with Maritime Telegraph and Telephone Company. I worked in the city of Halifax for the first few years of my career but later moved to the country to serve the small communities of northern Cape Breton, including Neil's Harbour, the place where it all began. When I left the city my supervisor shook my hand and said these cautionary words, "You know, Billy, you'll be working alone up there, with little or no supervision."

I smiled and said, "Yes, it's almost Paradise, isn't it?"

Many times over the years, I've admired the view from the top of a telephone pole. In particular, I've often been able to look out across the sea and find that small grey hump on the horizon that once was home. Sometimes, when the sea is calm and the air is clear it seems to reach out and beckon me.

Thirty-nine years have passed since we said farewell to St. Paul Island, and I have returned only a couple of times for brief visits. Both lighthouses on St. Paul Island have now succumbed to automation and the island is once again a place with no living human inhabitants. The tractor trail has been reclaimed by nature, impossible to locate unless one looks for subtle clues. The outbuildings on the Southwest light station have all collapsed, but the dwelling house itself is still standing, devoid of doors and windows. The kerosene-fired lighthouse has been replaced by a solar-powered light perched upon a fibreglass pedestal. Soon there will be nothing left of the old light station except the memory.

At this writing, the snow is blowing past the window outside my home in Ingonish. Thirty-eight miles across the sea on St. Paul Island, this same winter storm is raging. Tumultuous waves are being hurled against the cliffs, only to tumble back in noisy retreat as they have done for ten thousand years. Upstairs, in our crumbling home above the foamy turmoil, the wind-driven snow blows through the broken window panes and accumulates on my bedroom floor. And just maybe, in the quiet of the night, when moonlight shadows slant across the empty walls, the ghosts under the cellar floor still venture out and play in peaceful solitude.